STRANGER TO NOTHING

Philip Levine was born in 1928 in Detroit, where he studied at Wayne University. After working as a labourer, he settled in Fresno, California, and also lived in other countries for some time, including Spain. He taught at Fresno until his retirement, and now divides his time between Fresno and Brooklyn, New York. Levine has received many awards for his poetry, including the National Book Award (1980 & 1991), and the Pulitzer Prize in 1995 for *The Simple Truth*. He has published 16 collections of poems and two books of essays.

Stranger to Nothing: Selected Poems (Bloodaxe Books, 2006) is a Poetry Book Society Special Commendation. Covering the full range of his American collections, from *On the Edge* (1963) to *Breath* (2004), it is his first UK publication since an earlier *Selected Poems* was published by Secker & Warburg in 1984.

Philip Levine

STRANGER
TO NOTHING

SELECTED POEMS

BLOODAXE BOOKS

ISBN: 1 85224 737 1

First published 2006 by
Bloodaxe Books Ltd,
Highgreen,
Tarset,
Northumberland NE48 1RP.

www.bloodaxebooks.com
For further information about Bloodaxe titles
please visit our website or write to
the above address for a catalogue.

Bloodaxe Books Ltd acknowledges
the financial assistance of
Arts Council England, North East.

Cover printing by J. Thomson Colour Printers Ltd, Glasgow.

Printed in Great Britain by
Bell & Bain Limited, Glasgow, Scotland

for my sons
Theodore, John & Mark

ACKNOWLEDGEMENTS

This book contains poems selected from Philip Levine's American collections *On the Edge* (Stone Wall Press, 1963), *Not This Pig* (Wesleyan University Press, 1968), *Red Dust* (Kayak, 1971), *They Feed They Lion* (Atheneum, 1972), *1933* (Atheneum, 1974), *The Names of the Lost* (Atheneum, 1976), *7 Years from Somewhere* (Atheneum, 1979), *Ashes: Poems New and Old* (Atheneum, 1979), *One for the Rose* (Atheneum, 1981), *Sweet Will* (Atheneum, 1985) and *A Walk with Tom Jefferson* (Knopf, 1988), all these reprinted in *New Selected Poems* (Knopf, 1991), together with poems selected from *What Work Is* (1991), *The Simple Truth* (1994), *The Mercy* (1999) and *Breath* (2004), all published by Alfred A. Knopf.

Special thanks are due to Alfred A. Knopf (a division of Random House, Inc.) for their help in facilitating the publication of this book, and in particular to Deborah Garrison.

CONTENTS

For Fran

She packs the flower beds with leaves,
Rags, dampened papers, ties with twine
The lemon tree, but winter carves
Its features on the uprooted stem.

I see the true vein in her neck
And where the smaller ones have broken
Blueing the skin, and where the dark
Cold lines of weariness have eaten

Out through the winding of the bone.
On the hard ground where Adam strayed,
Where nothing but his wants remain,
What do we do to those we need,

To those whose need of us endures
Even the knowledge of what we are?
I turn to her whose future bears
The promise of the appalling air,

My living wife, Frances Levine,
Mother of Theodore, John, and Mark,
Out of whatever we have been
We will make something for the dark.

On the Edge

My name is Edgar Poe and I was born
In 1928 in Michigan.
Nobody gave a damn. The gruel I ate
Kept me alive, nothing kept me warm,
But I grew up, almost to five foot ten,
And nothing in the world can change my weight.

I have been watching you these many years,
There in the office, pencil poised and ready,
Or on the highway when you went ahead.
I did not write; I watched you watch the stars
Believing that the wheel of fate was steady;
I saw you rise from love and go to bed;

I heard you lie, even to your daughter.
I did not write, for I am Edgar Poe,
Edgar the mad one, silly, drunk, unwise,
But Edgar waiting on the edge of laughter,
And there is nothing that he does not know
Whose page is blanker than the raining skies.

The Horse

for Ichiro Kawamoto, humanitarian,
electrician, & survivor of Hiroshima

They spoke of the horse alive
without skin, naked, hairless,
without eyes and ears, searching
for the stableboy's caress.
Shoot it, someone said, but they
let him go on colliding with
tattered walls, butting his long
skull to pulp, finding no path
where iron fences corkscrewed in
the street and bicycles turned
like question marks.
                    Some fled and
some sat down. The river burned
all that day and into the
night, the stones sighed a moment
and were still, and the shadow
of a man's hand entered
a leaf.
        The white horse never
returned, and later they found
the stable boy, his back crushed
by a hoof, his mouth opened
around a cry that no one heard.

They spoke of the horse again
and again; their mouths opened
like the gills of a fish caught
above water.
              Mountain flowers
burst from the red clay walls, and
they said a new life was here.
Raw grass sprouted from the cobbles
like hair from a deafened ear.

The horse would never return.

There had been no horse. I could
tell from the way they walked
testing the ground for some cold
that the rage had gone out of
their bones in one mad dance.

A New Day

The headlights fading out at dawn,
A stranger at the shore, the shore
Not wakening to the great sea
Out of sleep, and night, and no sun
Rising where it rose before.

The old champion in a sweat suit
Tells me this is Chicago, this –
He does not say – is not the sea
But the chopped grey lake you get to
After travelling all night

From Dubuque, Cairo, or Wyandotte.
He takes off at a slow trot
And the fat slides under his shirt.
I recall the Friday night
In a beer garden in Detroit

I saw him flatten Ezzard Charles
On TV, and weep, and raise
Both gloved hands in a slow salute
To a God. I could tell him that.
I could tell him that those good days

Were no more and no less than these.
I could tell him that I thought
By now I must have reached the sea
We read about, or that last night
I saw a man break down and cry

Out of luck and out of gas
In Bruce's Crossing. We collect
Here at the shore, the two of us,
To make a pact, a people come
For a new world and a new home

And what we get is what we bring:
A grey light coming on at dawn,
No fresh start and no bird song
And no sea and no shore
That someone hasn't seen before.

Blasting from Heaven

The little girl won't eat her sandwich;
she lifts the bun and looks in, but the grey beef
    coated with relish is always there.
    Her mother says, 'Do it for mother.'
Milk and relish and a hard bun that comes off
    like a hat – a kid's life is a cinch.

And a mother's life? 'What can you do
with a man like that?' she asks the sleeping cook
    and then the old Negro who won't sit.
    'He's been out all night trying to get it.
I hope he gets it. What did he ever do
    but get it?' The Negro doesn't look,

though he looks like he's been out all night
trying. Everyone's been out all night trying.
    Why else would we be drinking beer
    at attention? If she were younger,
or if I were Prince Valiant, I would say that fate
    brought me here to quiet the crying,

to sweeten the sandwich of the child,
to waken the cook, to stop the Negro from
    bearing witness to the world. The dawn
    still hasn't come, and now we hear
the 8 o'clock whistles blasting from heaven,
    and with no morning the day is sold.

The Cemetery at Academy, California

On a hot summer Sunday
I came here with my children
who wandered among headstones
kicking up dust clouds. They found
a stone that said DAVI and
nothing more, and beneath the stone
a dead gopher, flat and dry.
Later they went off to play
on the dry dirt hills; I napped
under a great tree and woke
surprised by three teenagers.
They had put flowers in tin cans
around a headstone that showed
the sunrise over a slate sea,
and in the left-hand corner
a new bronze dove broke for peace.
Off in the distance my boys
had discovered the outhouses,
the twin whitewashed sentinels,
and were unwinding toilet
paper and dropping whatever
they could find through the dark holes
and when I found and scolded
them the two younger ones squeezed
my hands and walked stiffly at
my side past the three mourners.

I came here with a young girl
once who perched barefoot on her
family marker. 'I will go
there,' she said, 'next to my sister.'
It was early morning and
cold, and I wandered over
the pale clodded ground looking
for something rich or touching.
'It's all wildflowers in the spring,'
she had said, but in July
there were only the curled cut
flowers and the headstones blanked out
on the sun side, and the long
shadows deep as oil. I walked
to the sagging wire fence
that marked the margin of the

place and saw where the same ground,
festered here and there with reedy
grass, rose to a small knoll
and beyond where a windmill
held itself against the breeze.
I could hear her singing on
the stone under the great oak,
but when I got there she was
silent and I wasn't sure
and was ashamed to ask her,
ashamed that I had come here
where her people turned the earth.

Yet I came again, alone,
in the evening when the leaves
turned in the heat toward darkness
so late in coming. There was
her sister, there was her place
undisturbed, relatives and
friends, and other families
spread along the crests of this
burned hill. When I kneeled
to touch the ground it seemed like
something I had never seen,
the way the pale lumps broke down
to almost nothing, nothing
but the source of what they called
their living. She, younger now
than I, would be here some day
beneath the ground my hand combed.
The first night wind caught the leaves
above, crackling, and on
the trunk a salamander
faded in the fading light.
One comes for answers to a
place like this and finds even
in the darkness, even in
the sudden flooding of the
headlights, that in time one comes
to be a stranger to nothing.

Animals Are Passing from Our Lives

It's wonderful how I jog
on four honed-down ivory toes
my massive buttocks slipping
like oiled parts with each light step.

I'm to market. I can smell
the sour, grooved block, I can smell
the blade that opens the hole
and the pudgy white fingers

that shake out the intestines
like a hankie. In my dreams
the snouts drool on the marble,
suffering children, suffering flies,

suffering the consumers
who won't meet their steady eyes
for fear they could see. The boy
who drives me along believes

that any moment I'll fall
on my side and drum my toes
like a typewriter or squeal
and shit like a new housewife

discovering television,
or that I'll turn like a beast
cleverly to hook his teeth
with my teeth. No. Not this pig.

Baby Villon

He tells me in Bangkok he's robbed
Because he's white; in London because he's black;
In Barcelona, Jew; in Paris, Arab:
Everywhere and at all times, and he fights back.

He holds up seven thick little fingers
To show me he's rated seventh in the world,
And there's no passion in his voice, no anger
In the flat brown eyes flecked with blood.

He asks me to tell all I can remember
Of my father, his uncle; he talks of the war
In North Africa and what came after,
The loss of his father, the loss of his brother,

The windows of the bakery smashed and the fresh bread
Dusted with glass, the warm smell of rye
So strong he ate till his mouth filled with blood.
'Here they live, here they live and not die,'

And he points down at his black head ridged
With black kinks of hair. He touches my hair,
Tells me I should never disparage
The stiff bristles that guard the head of the fighter.

Sadly his fingers wander over my face,
And he says how fair I am, how smooth.
We stand to end this first and last visit.
Stiff, 116 pounds, five feet two,

No bigger than a girl, he holds my shoulders,
Kisses my lips, his eyes still open,
My imaginary brother, my cousin,
Myself made otherwise by all his pain.

Clouds

I

Dawn. First light tearing
at the rough tongues of the zinnias,
at the leaves of the just born.

Today it will rain. On the road
black cars are abandoned, but the clouds
ride above, their wisdom intact.

They are predictions. They never matter.
The jet fighters lift above the flat roofs,
black arrowheads trailing their future.

II

When the night comes small fires go out.
Blood runs to the heart and finds it locked.

Morning is exhaustion, tranquilisers, gasoline,
the screaming of frozen bearings,
the failures of will, the TV talking to itself.

The clouds go on eating oil, cigars,
housewives, sighing letters,
the breath of lies. In their great silent pockets
they carry off all our dead.

III

The clouds collect until there's no sky.
A boat slips its moorings and drifts
toward the open sea, turning and turning.

The moon bends to the canal and bathes
her torn lips, and the earth goes on
giving off her angers and sighs

and who knows or cares except these
breathing the first rains,
the last rivers running over iron.

IV

You cut an apple in two pieces
and ate them both. In the rain
the door knocked and you dreamed it.
On bad roads the poor walked under cardboard boxes.

The houses are angry because they're watched.
A soldier wants to talk with God
but his mouth fills with lost tags.

The clouds have seen it all, in the dark
they pass over the graves of the forgotten
and they don't cry or whisper.

They should be punished every morning,
they should be bitten and boiled like spoons.

Red Dust

This harpie with dry red curls
talked openly of her husband,
his impotence, his death, the death
of her lover, the birth and death
of her own beauty. She stared
into the mirror next to
our table littered with the wreck
of her appetite and groaned:
Look what you've done to me!
as though only that moment
she'd discovered her own face.
Look, and she shoved the burden
of her ruin on the waiter.

I do not believe in sorrow;
it is not American.
At 8,000 feet the towns
of this blond valley smoke
like the thin pipes of the Chinese,
and I go higher where the air
is clean, thin, and the underside
of light is clearer than the light.
Above the tree line the pines
crowd below like moments of the past
and on above the snow line
the cold underside of my arm,
the half in shadow, sweats with fear
as though it lay along the edge
of revelation.

And so my mind closes around
a square oil can crushed on the road
one morning, startled it was not
the usual cat. If a crow
had come out of the air to choose
its entrails could I have laughed?
If eagles formed now in the
shocked vegetation of my sight
would they be friendly? I can hear
their wings lifting them down, the feathers
tipped with red dust, that dust which
even here I taste, having eaten it
all these years.

A Sleepless Night

April, and the last of the plum blossoms
scatters on the black grass
before dawn. The sycamore, the lime,
the struck pine inhale
the first pale hints of sky.
                              An iron day,
I think, yet it will come
dazzling, the light
rise from the belly of leaves and pour
burning from the cups
of poppies.
                    The mockingbird squawks
from his perch, fidgets,
and settles back. The snail, awake
for good, trembles from his shell
and sets sail for China. My hand dances
in the memory of a million vanished stars.

A man has every place to lay his head.

Salami

Stomach of goat, crushed
sheep balls, soft full
pearls of pig eyes,
snout gristle, fresh earth,
worn iron of trotter, slate
of Zaragoza, dried cat heart,
cock claws. She grinds
them with one hand and
with the other fists
mountain thyme, basil,
paprika, and knobs of garlic.
And if a tooth of stink thistle
pulls blood from the round
blue marbled hand
all the better for
this ruby of Pamplona,
this bright jewel of Vich,
this stained crown
of Solsona, this
salami.
            The daughter
of mismatched eyes,
36 year old infant smelling
of milk. Mama, she cries, mama,
but mama is gone,
and the old stone-cutter
must wipe the drool
from her jumper. His puffed fingers
unbutton and point her
to toilet. Ten, twelve hours
a day, as long as the winter sun
holds up he rebuilds
the unvisited church
of San Martín. Cheep cheep
of the hammer high above
the town, sparrow cries
lost in the wind or lost
in the mind. At dusk he leans
to the coal dull wooden Virgin

24

and asks for blessings on
the slow one and peace
on his grizzled head, asks
finally and each night
for the forbidden, for
the knowledge of every
mysterious stone, and
the words go out on
the overwhelming incense
of salami.
         A single crow
passed high over the house,
I wakened out of nightmare.
The winds had changed,
the Tramontana was tearing
out of the Holy Mountains
to meet the sea winds
in my yard, burning and
scaring the young pines.
The single poplar wailed
in terror. With salt,
with guilt, with the need
to die, the vestments
of my life flared, I
was on fire, a stranger
staggering through my house
butting walls and falling
over furniture, looking
for a way out. In the last room
where moonlight slanted
through a broken shutter
I found my smallest son
asleep or dead, floating
on a bed of colorless light.
When I leaned closer
I could smell the small breaths
going and coming, and each
bore its prayer for me,
the true and earthy prayer
of salami.

Saturday Sweeping

Saturday sweeping
with an old broom
counting the strokes
back and forth.
The dust sprays
up silver in the
February sun
and comes down gray.
Soft straw muzzle
poking in and
bringing out
scraps of news,
little fingers
and signatures.
Everybody's
had this room
one time or another
and never thought
to sweep. Outside
the snows stiffen,
the roofs loosen
their last teeth
into the streets.
Outside it's
1952,
Detroit, unburned,
stumbles away
from my window
over the drained roofs
toward the river
to scald its useless
hands. Half
the men in this town
are crying in
the snow, their eyes
blackened like
Chinese soldiers.
The gates are closing
at Dodge Main
and Wyandotte
Chemical; they
must go home
to watch the kids

scrub their brown
faces or grease
cartridges for
the showdown.
If anyone knocks
on your door
he'll be
oil flecked or
sea born, he'll
be bringing word
from the people
of the ice drifts
or the great talking dogs
that saved the Jews.
Meanwhile our masters
will come on
television
to ask for our help.
Here, the radiator's
working, stove says
Don't touch,
and the radio's crying,
I don't get enough.
I'm my keeper,
the only thing
I've got,
sweeping out
my one-room life
while the sun's
still up.

Angel Butcher

At sun up I am up
hosing down the outdoor abattoir
getting ready. The water
steams and hisses on the white stones
and the air pales to a
thin blue.
           Today it is
Christophe. I don't see him
come up the long climb or
know he's here until I hear
my breathing double
and he's beside me smiling
like a young girl.
             He asks
me the names of all
the tools and all
their functions, he lifts
and weighs and
balances, and runs a long
forefinger down the tongue
of each blade.
           He asks
me how I came to this place and
this work, and I tell him how
I began with animals, and
he tells me how
he began with animals. We
talk about growing up and losing
the strange things we never
understood and settling.
           I help
him with his robes; he
has a kind of modesty and sits
on the stone table with
the ends of the gown crossed
in his lap.
           He wants to die
like a rabbit, and he wants me
to help him. I hold
his wrist; it's small, like
the throat of a young hen, but
cool and dry. He holds
mine and I can feel the

blood thudding in the ring
his fingers make.
                    He helps me, he
guides my hand at first. I can
feel my shoulders settle and
the bones take the weight, I can
feel my lungs flower as the
swing begins. He smiles again
with only one side of his mouth
and looks down to the
dark valley where the cities
burn. When I hit
him he comes apart like a
perfect puzzle or an
old flower.
                    And my legs
dance and twitch for hours.

They Feed They Lion

Out of burlap sacks, out of bearing butter,
Out of black bean and wet slate bread,
Out of the acids of rage, the candor of tar,
Out of creosote, gasoline, drive shafts, wooden dollies,
They Lion grow.
        Out of the gray hills
Of industrial barns, out of rain, out of bus ride,
West Virginia to Kiss My Ass, out of buried aunties,
Mothers hardening like pounded stumps, out of stumps,
Out of the bones' need to sharpen and the muscles' to stretch,
They Lion grow.
        Earth is eating trees, fence posts,
Gutted cars, earth is calling in her little ones,
'Come home, Come home!' From pig balls,
From the ferocity of pig driven to holiness,
From the furred ear and the full jowl come
The repose of the hung belly, from the purpose
They Lion grow.
        From the sweet glues of the trotters
Come the sweet kinks of the fist, from the full flower
Of the hams the thorax of caves,
From 'Bow Down' come 'Rise Up',
Come they Lion from the reeds of shovels,
The grained arm that pulls the hands,
They Lion grow.
        From my five arms and all my hands,
From all my white sins forgiven, they feed,
From my car passing under the stars,
They Lion, from my children inherit,
From the oak turned to a wall, they Lion,
From they sack and they belly opened
And all that was hidden burning on the oil-stained earth
They feed they Lion and he comes.

To P.L., 1916-1937

a soldier of the Republic

Gray earth peeping through snow,
you lay for three days
with one side of your face
frozen to the ground. They tied your cheek
with the red and black scarf
of the Anarchists, and bundled you
in canvas, and threw you away.
Before that an old country woman
of the Aragon, spitting on her thumb,
rubbing it against her forefinger,
stole your black Wellingtons,
the gray hunting socks, and the long
slender knife you wore
in a little leather scabbard
riding your right hip. She honed it,
ran her finger down the blade, and laughed,
though she had no meat to cut,
blessing your tight fists
that had fallen side by side
like frozen faces on your hard belly
that was becoming earth. (Years later
she saw the two faces
at table, and turned from the bread
and the steaming oily soup, turned
to the darkness of the open door,
and opened her eyes to darkness
that they might be filled with anything
but those two faces squeezed
in the blue of snow and snow and snow.)
She blessed your feet, still pink,
with hard yellow shields of skin
at heel and toe, and she laughed
scampering across the road, into
the goat field, and up the long hill,
the boots bundled in her skirts,
and the gray hunting socks, and the knife.
For seven weeks she wore the boots
stuffed with rags at toe and heel.
She thought she understood
why you lay down to rest
even in snow, and gave them to a nephew,
and the gray socks too.

The knife is still used, the black handle
almost white, the blade
worn thin since there is meat to cut.
Without laughter she is gone
ten years now,
and on the road to Huesca in spring
there is no one to look for you
among the wild jonquils, the curling
grasses at the road side,
and the blood red poppies, no one
to look on the farthest tip
of wind breathing down from the mountains
and shaking the stunted pines you hid among.

Breath

Who hears the humming
of rocks at great height,
the long steady drone
of granite holding together,
the strumming of obsidian
to itself? I go among
the stones stooping
and pecking like a
sparrow, imagining
the glacier's final push
resounding still. In
a freezing mountain
stream, my hand opens
scratched and raw and
flutters strangely,
more like an animal
or wild blossom in wind
than any part of me. Great
fields of stone
stretching away under
a slate sky, their single
flower the flower
of my right hand.
                         Last night
the fire died into itself
black stick by stick
and the dark came out
of my eyes flooding
everything. I
slept alone and dreamed
of you in an old house
back home among
your country people,
among the dead, not
any living one besides
yourself. I woke
scared by the gasping
of a wild one, scared
by my own breath, and
slowly calmed
remembering your weight
beside me all these
years, and here and

there an eye of stone
gleamed with the warm light
of an absent star.
                    Today
in this high clear room
of the world, I squat
to the life of rocks
jewelled in the stream
or whispering
like shards. What fears
are still held locked
in the veins till the last
fire, and who will calm
us then under a gold sky
that will be all of earth?
Two miles below on the burning
summer plains, you go
about your life one
more day. I give you
almond blossoms
for your hair, your hair
that will be white, I give
the world my worn-out breath
on an old tune, I give
it all I have
and take it back again.

Zaydee

Why does the sea burn? Why do the hills cry?
My grandfather opens a fresh box
of English Ovals, lights up, and lets the smoke
drift like clouds from his lips.

Where did my father go in my fifth autumn?
In the blind night of Detroit
on the front porch, Grandfather points up
at a constellation shaped like a cock and balls.

A tiny man, at 13 I outgrew his shirts.
I then beheld a closet of stolen suits,
a hive of elevator shoes, crisp hankies,
new bills in the cupboard, old in the wash.

I held the spotted hands that passed over
the breasts of airlines stewardesses,
that moved in the fields like a wind
stirring the long hairs of grain.

Where is the ocean? the flying fish?
the God who speaks from a cloud?
He carries a card-table out under the moon
and plays gin rummy and cheats.

He took me up in his arms
when I couldn't walk and carried me
into the grove where the bees sang
and the stream paused forever.

He laughs in the movies, cries in the streets,
the judges in their gowns are monkeys,
the lawyers mice, a cop is a fat hand.
He holds up a strawberry and bites it.

He sings a song of freestone peaches
all in a box,
in the street he sings out Idaho potatoes
California, California oranges.

He sings the months in prison,
sings salt pouring down the sunlight,
shovelling all night in the stove factory
he sings the oven breathing fire.

Where did he go when his autumn came?
He sat before the steering wheel
of the black Packard, he turned the key,
pressed the starter, and he went.

The maples blazed golden and red
a moment and then were still,
the long streets were still and the snow
swirled where I lay down to rest.

Grandmother in Heaven

Darkness gathering in the branches
of the elm, the car lights going home,

someone's beautiful Polish daughter
with a worn basket of spotted eggs,

an elbow of cabbage, carrots, leaves,
chicken claws scratching the air,

she comes up the cracked walk to the stairway
of shadows and lost dolls and lost breath.

Beautiful Polish daughter with hands
as round and white as buns, daughter

of no lights in the kitchen, no one sits
on the sofa, no one dreams in the tub,

she in her empty room in heaven
unpacking the basket piece by piece

on the silent, enamelled table
with a little word for each, a curse

for the bad back and the black radish
and three quick spits for the pot.

The Poem Circling Hamtramck, Michigan, All Night in Search of You

He hasn't gone to work,
he'll never go back to work.
The wife has gone home, mad,
with the baby on one arm.
Swaying on his good leg,
he calls out to the bare bulb
a name and opens his arms.
The old woman,
the beer gone from her glass,
turns back to the bar.
She's seen them before
with hard, knotted bellies,
with the bare white breasts of boys.
How many times has she stared
into those eyes glistening
with love or pain
and seen nothing
but love or pain.
Deep at night, when she
was coldest, he would always
rise and dress so as not
to miss the first streetcar
burning homeward, and she
would rock alone toward dawn.

If someone would enter now
and take these lovers – for they
are lovers – in his arms
and rock them together
like a mother with a child
in each arm, this man
with so much desire, this woman
with none, then it would not be
Hamtramck, it would not be
this night. They know it
and wait, he staring
into the light, she into
the empty glass. In the darkness
of this world men
pull on heavy canvas gloves,
dip into rubber coats

and enter the fires. The rats
frozen under the conveyors
turn to let their eyes
fill with dawn. A strange star
is born one more time.

Uncle

I remember the forehead born
before Abraham
and flecked with white paint,
the two hands kneading
each other at the sink.
In the basement on Grand
he showed me
his radio,
Manila, Atlantis,
the cities of the burning plains,
the coupons
in comic books, the ads of the air.
Prophet of burned cars
and broken fans, he taught
the toilet the eternal,
argued the Talmud
under his nails. The long boats
with the names of winds
set sail
in the sea of his blind eye.

How could he come
humpbacked
in his crisp undershirt
on the front porch in black Detroit
bringing in the milk,
the newspaper, the bills
long past noon? His truck howls
all night to Benton Harbor, Saginaw,
Dog of the Prairie.
In the high work camps
the men break toward dawn.
He sleeps under a mountain.
Uncle, I call you again Uncle,
I come too late
with a bottle of milk
and a chipped cup of Schnapps
to loosen your fever, undo
your arms and legs
so you can rise
above Belle Isle and the Straits,
your clear eye
rid of our rooms forever,
the glass of fat the blue flame.

1933

My father entered the kingdom of roots
    his head as still as a stone
    (Laid out in black with a white tie
    he blinked
    and I told no one
    except myself over and over)
    laid out long and gray

The hands that stroked my head
    the voice in the dark asking
    he drove the car all the way to the river
      where the ships burned
    he rang with keys and coins
    he knew the animals and their names
      touched the nose of the horse
      and kicked the German dog away
    he brought Ray Estrada from Mexico in his 16th year
      scolded him like a boy, gave him beer money
      and commanded him to lift and push
    he left in October without his hat
    who answered to the name Father

Father, the world is different in many places
    the old Ford Trimotors are gone to scrap
    the Terraplane turned to snow
    four armies passed over your birthplace
      your house is gone
      all your tall sisters gone
      your fathers
      everyone
    Roosevelt ran again
    you would still be afraid

You would not know me now, I have a son taller than you
    I feel the first night winds catch in the almond
      the plum bend
      and I go in afraid of the death you are
    I climb the tree in the vacant lot
      and leave the fruit untasted
    I blink the cold winds in from the sea
      walking with Teddy, my little one
      squeezing his hand I feel his death
    I find the glacier and wash my face in Arctic dust

I shit handfuls of earth
I stand in the spring river pissing at stars
I see the diamondback at the end of the path
    hissing and rattling
    and will not shoot

The sun is gone, the moon is a slice of hope
    the stars are burned eyes that see
    the wind is the breath of the ocean
    the death of the fish is the allegory
        you slice it open and spill the entrails
        you remove the spine
        the architecture of the breast
        you slap it home
        the oils snap and sizzle
        you live in the world
    you eat all the unknown deeps
    the great sea oaks rise from the floor
    the bears dip their paws in clear streams
        they hug their great matted coats
        and laugh in the voices of girls
    a man drops slowly like brandy or glue

In the cities of the world
    the streets darken with flies
    all the dead fathers fall out of heaven
        and begin again
    the angel of creation is a sparrow in the roadway
    storks rise slowly pulling the houses after them
    butterflies eat away the eyes of the sun
    the last ashes off the fire of the brain
    the last leavening of snow
    grains of dirt torn from under fingernails and eyes
    you drink these

There is the last darkness burning itself to death
    there are nine women come in the dawn with pitchers
    there is my mother
        a dark child in the schoolyard
        miles from anyone
    she has begun to bleed as her mother did
    there is my brother, the first born, the mild one
        his cold breath fogging the bombsight
    there is the other in his LTD
        he talks to the phone, he strokes his thighs
        he dismisses me

my mother waits for the horsecart to pass
my mother prays to become fat and wise
    she becomes fat and wise
the cat dies and it rains
the dog groans by the side door
the old hen flies up in a spasm of gold

My woman gets out of bed in the dark and washes her face
    she goes to the kitchen before we waken
    she picks up a skillet, an egg
    the kids go off to school without socks
    in the rain the worms come out to live
    my father opens the telegram under the moon
        Cousin Philip is dead
        my father stands on the porch in his last summer
        he holds back his tears
        he holds back my tears

Once in childhood the stars held still all night
    the moon swelled like a plum but white and silken
    the last train from Chicago howled through the ghetto
    I came downstairs
    my father sat writing in a great black book
    a pile of letters
    a pile of checks
    (he would pay his debts)
    the moon would die
    the stars jelly
    the sea freeze
    I would be a boy in worn shoes splashing through rain

Belle Isle, 1949

We stripped in the first warm spring night
and ran down into the Detroit River
to baptise ourselves in the brine
of car parts, dead fish, stolen bicycles,
melted snow. I remember going under
hand in hand with a Polish highschool girl
I'd never seen before, and the cries
our breath made caught at the same time
on the cold, and rising through the layers
of darkness into the final moonless atmosphere
that was this world, the girl breaking
the surface after me and swimming out
on the starless waters towards the lights
of Jefferson Ave. and the stacks
of the old stove factory unwinking.
Turning at last to see no island at all
but a perfect calm dark as far
as there was sight, and then a light
and another riding low out ahead
to bring us home, ore boats maybe, or smokers
walking alone. Back panting
to the gray coarse beach we didn't dare
fall on, the damp piles of clothes,
and dressing side by side in silence
to go back where we came from.

New Season

My son and I go walking in the garden.
It is April 12, Friday, 1974.
Teddy points to the slender trunk
of the plum and recalls the digging
last fall through three feet
of hardpan and opens his palms
in the brute light of noon, the heels
glazed with callus, the long fingers
thicker than mine and studded with
silver rings. My mother is 70 today.
He flicks two snails off a leaf
and smashes them underfoot
on the red brick path. Saturday,
my wife stood here, her cheek cut
by a scar of dirt, dirt on her bare
shoulders, on the brown belly,
damp and sour in the creases
of her elbows. She held up a parsnip
squat, misshapen, a tooth pulled
from the earth, and laughed
her great white laugh. Teddy talks
of the wars of the young, Larry V.
and Ricky's brother in the movies,
on Belmont, at McDonald's,
ready to fight for nothing, hard,
redded or on air, 'low riders,
grease, what'd you say about my mama!'
Home late, one in the back seat,
his fingers broken, eyes welling
with pain, the eyes and jawbones
swollen and rough. 70 today, the woman
who took my hand and walked me
past the corridor of willows
to the dark pond where the one swan
drifted. I start to tell him
and stop, the story of my 15th spring.
That a sailor had thrown a black baby
off the Belle Isle Bridge was
the first lie we heard, and the city
was at war for real. We would waken
the next morning to find Sherman tanks
at the curb and soldiers camped
on the lawns. Damato said he was

45

'goin downtown bury a hatchet
in a nigger's head'. Women
took coffee and milk to the soldiers
and it was one long block party
till the trucks and tanks loaded up
and stumbled off. No one saw
Damato for a week, and when I did
he was slow, head down, his right am
blooming in a great white bandage.
He said nothing. On mornings I rise
early, I watch my son in the bathroom,
shirtless, thick-armed and hard,
working with brush and comb
at his full blond head that suddenly
curled like mine and won't
come straight. 7 years passed
before Della Daubien told me
how three white girls from the shop
sat on her on the Woodward streetcar
so the gangs couldn't find her
and pull her off like they did
the black janitor and beat
an eye blind. She would never
forget, she said, and her old face
glows before me in shame
and terror. Tonight, after dinner,
after the long, halting call
to my mother, I'll come out here
to the yard rinsed in moonlight
that blurs it all. She will not
become the small openings
in my brain again through which the wind
rages, though she was the ocean
that ebbed in my blood, the storm clouds
that battered my lungs, though I hide
in the crotch of the orange tree
and weep where the future grows
like a scar, she will not come again
in the brilliant day. My cat Nellie,
15 now, follows me, safe
in the dark from mockingbird
and jay, her fur frost tipped
in the pure air, and together we hear
the wounding of the rose, the willow
on fire – to the dark pond
where the one swan drifted, the woman

is 70 now – the willow is burning,
the rhododendrons shrivel
like paper under water, all
the small secret mouths are feeding
on the green heart of the plum.

Wednesday

I could say the day began
behind the Sierras,
in the orange grove the ladder
that reaches partway
to the stars grew
a shadow, and the fruit
wet with mist put on
its color and glowed
like a globe of fire,
and when I wakened
I was alone and the room
still, the white walls,
the white ceiling, the stained
wood floor held me until
I sat up and reached out
first for a glass
of stale water to free
my tongue, and then
the wristwatch purchased
before you were born,
and while the leaves ticked
against the window and
the dust rose golden
in the chalice of the air
I gave you this name.

On the Murder of Lieutenant José del Castillo by the Falangist Bravo Martinez, July 12, 1936

When the Lieutenant of the Guardia de Asalto
heard the automatic go off, he turned
and took the second shot just above
the sternum, the third tore away
the right shoulder of his uniform,
the fourth perforated his cheek. As he
slid out of his comrade's hold
toward the gray cement of the Ramblas
he lost count and knew only
that he would not die and that the blue sky
smudged with clouds was not heaven
for heaven was nowhere and in his eyes
slowly filling with their own light.
The pigeons that spotted the cold floor
of Barcelona rose as he sank below
the waves of silence crashing
on the far shores of his legs, growing
faint and watery. His hands opened
a last time to receive the benedictions
of automobile exhaust and rain
and the rain of soot. His mouth,
that would never again say 'I am afraid',
closed on nothing. The old grandfather
hawking daisies at his stand pressed
a handkerchief against his lips
and turned his eyes away before they held
the eyes of a gunman. The shepherd dogs
on sale howled in their cages
and turned in circles. There is more
to be said, but by someone who has suffered
and died for his sister the earth
and his brothers the beasts and the trees.
The Lieutenant can hear it, the prayer
that comes on the voices of water, today
or yesterday, from Chicago or Valladolid,
and hangs like smoke above this street
he won't walk as a man ever again.

And the Trains Go On

We stood at the back door
of the shop in the night air
while a line of box cars
of soured wheat and pop bottles
uncoupled and was sent creaking
down our spur. Once, when I
unsealed a car and the two
of us strained the door open
with a groan of rust, an old man
stepped out and tipped his hat.
'It's all yours, boys!'
and he went off, stiff-legged,
smelling of straw and shit.
I often wonder whose father
he was and how long he kept
moving until the police
found him, ticketless, sleeping
in a 2nd class waiting room
and tore the cardboard box
out of his hands and beat him
until the ink of his birth smudged
and surrendered its separate vowels.
In the great railyard of Milano
the dog with the white throat
and the soiled muzzle crossed
and recrossed the tracks
'searching for his master',
said the boy, but his grandfather
said, 'No. He was sent by God
to test the Italian railroads.'
When I lie down at last to sleep
inside a boxcar of coffins bound
for the villages climbing north
will I waken in a small station
where women have come to claim
what is left of glory? Or will
I sleep until the silver bridge
spanning the Mystic River jabs
me awake, and I am back
in a dirty work shirt that says *Phil*,
24 years old, hungry and lost, on
the run from a war no one can win?
I want to travel one more time

with the wind whipping in
the open door, with you to keep
me company, back the long
tangled road that leads us home.
Through Flat Rock going east
picking up speed, the damp fields
asleep in moonlight. You stand
beside me, breathing the cold
in silence. When you grip
my arm hard and lean way out
and shout out the holy names
of the lost neither of us is scared
and our tears mean nothing.

To My God in His Sickness

1

A boy is as old as the stars
that will not answer
as old as the last snows
that blacken his hands
though he wakes at 3
and goes to the window
where the crooked fence is blessed
and the long Packard
and the bicycle wheel
though he walk the streets
warm in the halo of his breath
and is blessed over and over
he will waken in the slow dawn
he will call his uncles out
from the sad bars of Irish statesmen
all the old secret reds
who pledge in the park
and raise drinks
and remember Spain

Though he honor the tree
the sierra of snow
the stream that died years ago
though he honor his breakfast
the water in his glass
the bear in his belly
though he honor all crawling
and winged things
the man in his glory
the woman in her salt
though he savor the cup of filth
though he savor Lake Erie
savor the rain burning down
on Gary, Detroit, Wheeling
though my grandmother argues
the first cause of night
and the kitchen cantor mumbles his names
still the grave will sleep

I came this way before
my road ran by your house
crowded with elbows of mist

and pots banging to be filled
my coat was the colors of rain
and six gray sparrows sang
on the branches of my grave

2

A rabbit snared in a fence of pain
screams and screams
I waken, a child again
and answer
I answer my father
hauling his stone up the last few breaths
I answer Moses bumbling before you
the cat circling three times
before she stretches out and yawns
the mole gagged on fresh leaves

In Folsom, Jaroubi, alone before dawn
remembers the long legs of a boy
his own once and now his son's
Billy Ray holds my hand to his heart
in the black and white still photograph
of the exercise yard
in the long shadows of the rifle towers
we say goodbye forever
Later, at dusk the hills
across the dry riverbed
hold the last light
long after it's gone
and glow like breath

I wake
and it's not a dream
I see the long coast of the continent
writhing in sleep
this America we thought we dreamed
falling away flake by flake
into the sea
and the sea blackening and burning

I see a man curled up, the size of an egg
I see a woman hidden in a carburetor
a child reduced to one word
crushed under an airmail stamp
or a cigarette

Can the hands rebuild the rocks
can the tongue make air or water
can the blood flow back
into the twigs of the child
can the clouds take back their deaths

3

First light of morning
it is the world again
the domed hills across the gorge
take the air slowly
the day will be hot and long
Jimmy Ray, Gordon, Jaroubi
all the prisoners have been awake
for hours remembering
I walk through the dense brush
down to the river
that descended all night from snow
small stones worn away
old words, lost truths
ground to their essential nonsense
I lift you in my hand
and inhale, the odor of light
out of darkness, substance out of air
of blood before it reddens and runs

When I first knew you
I was a friend to the ox and walked
with Absalom and raised my hand
against my hand
and died for want of you
and turned to stone and air and water
the answer to my father's tears

Starlight

My father stands in the warm evening
on the porch of my first house.
I am four years old and growing tired.
I see his head among the stars,
the glow of his cigarette, redder
than the summer moon riding
low over the old neighborhood. We
are alone, and he asks me if I am happy.
'Are you happy?' I cannot answer.
I do not really understand the word,
and the voice, my father's voice, is not
his voice, but somehow thick and choked,
a voice I have not heard before, but
heard often since. He bends and passes
a thumb beneath each of my eyes.
The cigarette is gone, but I can smell
the tiredness that hangs on his breath.
He has found nothing, and he smiles
and holds my head with both his hands.
Then he lifts me to his shoulder,
and now I too am there among the stars
as tall as he. Are you happy? I say.
He nods in answer, Yes! oh yes! oh yes!
And in that new voice he says nothing,
holding my head tight against his head,
his eyes closed up against the starlight,
as though those tiny blinking eyes
of light might find a tall, gaunt child
holding his child against the promises
of autumn, until the boy slept
never to waken in that world again.

On a Drawing by Flavio

Above my desk
the Rabbi of Auschwitz
bows his head and prays
for us all, and the earth
which long ago inhaled
his last flames turns
its face toward the light.
Outside the low trees
take the first gray shapes.
At the cost of such
death must I enter
this body again,
this body which is
itself closing on
death? Now the sun
rises above a stunning
valley, and the orchards
thrust their burning
branches into the day.
Do as you please, says
the sun without uttering
a word. But I can't.
I am this hand that
would raise itself
against the earth
and I am the earth too.
I look again and closer
at the Rabbi and at last
see he has my face
that opened its eyes
so many years ago
to death. He has these
long tapering fingers
that long ago reached
for our father's hand
long gone to dirt, these
fingers that hold
hand to forearm,
forearm to hand because
that is all that God
gave us to hold.

Ashes

Far off, from the burned fields
of cotton, smoke rises and scatters
on the last winds of afternoon.
The workers have come in hours ago,
and nothing stirs. The old bus creaked
by full of faces wide-eyed with hunger.
I sat wondering how long the earth
would let the same children die day
after day, let the same women curse
their precious hours, the same men bow
to earn our scraps. I only asked.
And now the answer batters the sky:
with fire there is smoke, and after, ashes.
You can howl your name into the wind
and it will blow it into dust, you
can pledge your single life, the earth
will eat it all, the way you eat
an apple, meat, skin, core, seeds.
Soon the darkness will fall on all
the tired bodies of those who have
torn our living from the silent earth,
and they can sleep and dream of sleep
without end, but before first light
bloodies the sky opening in the east
they will have risen one by one
and dressed in clothes still hot
and damp. Before I waken they are
already bruised by the first hours
of the new sun. The same men
who were never boys, the same women
their faces gone gray with anger,
and the children who will say nothing.
Do you want the earth to be heaven?
Then pray, go down on your knees
as though a king stood before you,
and pray to become all you'll
never be, a drop of sea water,
a small hurtling flame across the sky,
a fine flake of dust that moves
at evening like smoke at great height
above the earth and sees it all.

Francisco, I'll Bring You Red Carnations

Here in the great cemetery
behind the fortress of Barcelona
I have come once more to see
the graves of my fallen.
Two ancient picnickers direct
us down the hill. 'Durruti,'
says the man, 'I was on
his side.' The woman hushes
him. All the way down
this is a city of the dead,
871,251 *difuntos*.
The poor packed in tenements
a dozen high; the rich
in splendid homes or temples.
So nothing has changed
except for the single
unswerving fact: they are
all dead. Here is the Plaza
of San Jaime, here the Rambla
of San Pedro, so every death
still has a mailing address,
but since this is Spain
the mail never comes or
comes too late to be of use.
Between the cemetery and
the Protestant burial ground
we find the three stones
all in a row: Ferrer Guardia,
B. Durruti, F. Ascaso, the names
written with marking pens,
and a few circled A's and tributes
to the FAI and CNT.
For two there are floral
displays, but Ascaso faces
eternity with only a stone.
Maybe as it should be. He was
a stone, a stone and a blade,
the first grinding and sharpening
the other. Half his 36

years were spent in prisons
or on the run, and yet
in that last photograph
taken less than an hour before
he died, he stands in a dark
suit, smoking, a rifle slung
behind his shoulder, and glances
sideways at the camera
half smiling. It is July 20,
1936, and before the darkness
falls a darkness will have
fallen on him. While
the streets are echoing
with victory and revolution,
Francisco Ascaso will take up
the hammered little blade
of his spirit and enter for
the last time the republics
of death. I remember
his words to a frightened
comrade who questioned
the wisdom of attack: 'We
have gathered here to die, but we
don't have to die with dogs,
so go.' Forty-one years
ago, and now the city stretches
as far as the eye can see,
huge cement columns like nails
pounded into the once green
meadows of the Llobregat.
Your Barcelona is gone,
the old town swallowed
in industrial filth and
the burning mists of gasoline.
Only the police remain, armed
and arrogant, smiling masters
of the boulevards, the police
and your dream of the city
of God, where every man
and every woman gives
and receives the gifts of work
and care, and that dream
goes on in spite of slums,
in spite of death clouds,
the roar of trucks, the harbor
staining the mother sea,

it goes on in spite of all
that mocks it. We have it here
growing in our hearts, as
your comrade said, and when
we give it up with our last
breaths someone will gasp
it home to their lives.
Francisco, stone, knife blade,
single soldier still on
the run down the darkest
street of all, we will be back
across an ocean and a continent
to bring you red carnations,
to celebrate the unbroken
promise of your life that
once was frail and flesh.

Milkweed

Remember how unimportant
they seemed, growing loosely
in the open fields we crossed
on the way to school. We
would carve wooden swords
and slash at the luscious trunks
until the white milk started
and then flowed. Then we'd
go on to the long day after
day of the History of History
or the tables of numbers and order
as the clock slowly paid
out the moments. The windows
went dark first with rain
and then snow, and then the days,
then the years ran together and not
one mattered more than
another, and not one mattered.

Two days ago I walked
the empty woods, bent over,
crunching through oak leaves,
asking myself questions
without answers. From somewhere
a froth of seeds drifted by touched
with gold in the last light
of a lost day, going with
the wind as they always did.

The Last Step

Once I was a small grain
of fire burning on the rim
of day, and I waited in silence
until the dawn released me
and I climbed into the light.
Here, in the brilliant orchard,
the thick-skinned oranges
doze in winter light,
late roses shred the wind,
and blood rains into
the meadows of winter grass.

I thought I would find my father
and hand in hand we would pace off
a child's life, I thought the air,
crystal around us, would hold
his words until they became
me, never to be forgotten.
I thought the rain was far off
under another sky. I thought
that to become a man I
had only to wait, and the years,
gathering slowly, would take me there.

They took me somewhere else.
The twisted fig tree, the almond,
not yet white crowned, the slow
tendrils of grape reaching
into the sky are companions
for a time, but nothing goes
the whole way. Not even the snail
smeared to death on a flat rock
or the tiny sparrow fallen from
the nest and flaring the yellow grass.
The last step, like an entrance,
is alone, in darkness, and without song.

Let Me Begin Again

Let me begin again as a speck
of dust caught in the night winds
sweeping out to sea. Let me begin
this time knowing the world is
salt water and dark clouds, the world
is grinding and sighing all night, and dawn
comes slowly and changes nothing. Let
me go back to land after a lifetime
of going nowhere. This time lodged
in the feathers of some scavenging gull
white above the black ship that docks
and broods upon the oily waters of
your harbor. This leaking freighter
has brought a hold full of hayforks
from Spain, great jeroboams of dark
Algerian wine and quill pens that can't
write English. The sailors have stumbled
off toward the bars or the bright houses.
The captain closes his log and falls asleep.
1/10'28. Tonight I shall enter my life
after being at sea for ages, quietly,
in a hospital named for an automobile.
The one child of millions of children
who has flown alone by the stars
above the black wastes of moonless waters
that stretched forever, who has turned
golden in the full sun of a new day.
A tiny wise child who this time will love
his life because it is like no other.

You Can Have It

My brother comes home from work
and climbs the stairs to our room.
I can hear the bed groan and his shoes drop
one by one. You can have it, he says.

The moonlight streams in the window
and his unshaven face is whitened
like the face of the moon. He will sleep
long after noon and waken to find me gone.

Thirty years will pass before I remember
that moment when suddenly I knew each man
has one brother who dies when he sleeps
and sleeps when he rises to face this life,

and that together they are only one man
sharing a heart that always labours, hands
yellowed and cracked, a mouth that gasps
for breath and asks, Am I gonna make it?

All night at the ice plant he had fed
the chute its silvery blocks, and then I
stacked cases of orange soda for the children
of Kentucky, one gray boxcar at a time

with always two more waiting. We were twenty
for such a short time and always in
the wrong clothes, crusted with dirt
and sweat. I think now we were never twenty.

In 1948 the city of Detroit, founded
by de la Mothe Cadillac for the distant purposes
of Henry Ford, no one wakened or died,
no one walked the streets or stoked a furnace,

for there was no such year, and now
that year has fallen off all the old newspapers,
calendars, doctors' appointments, bonds,
wedding certificates, drivers' licenses.

The city slept. The snow turned to ice.
The ice to standing pools or rivers
racing in the gutters. Then bright grass rose
between the thousands of cracked squares,

and that grass died. I give you back 1948.
I give you all the years from then
to the coming one. Give me back the moon
with its frail light falling across a face.

Give me back my young brother, hard
and furious, with wide shoulders and a curse
for God and burning eyes that look upon
all creation and say, You can have it.

I Was Born in Lucerne

Everyone says otherwise. They take me
to a flat on Pingree in Detroit
and say, Up there, the second floor. I say,
No, in a small Italian hotel overlooking
the lake. No doctor, no nurse. Just
a beautiful single woman who preferred
to remain that way and raise me to
the proper height, weight, and level of audacity.
They show me a slip of paper that says,
'Ford Hospital, Dr Smear, male', and all
the rest of the clichés I could have lived by.
All that afternoon my mother held me close
to her side and watched the slow fog lift
and the water and sky blue all at once,
then darken to a deeper blue that turned
black at last, as I faced the longest night
of my life with tight fists and closed eyes
beside a woman of independence and courage
who sang the peasant songs of her region.
Later she recited the names of small mountain
villages like a litany that would protect
us against the rise of darkness and the fall
of hundreds of desperate men no longer
willing to pull in the fields or the factories
of Torino for a few lire and a Thank You.
She told me of those men, my uncles
and cousins, with names like water pouring
from stone jugs. Primo Grunwald,
Carlo Finzi, Mario Antonio Todesco, Beniamino
Levi, my grandfather. They would die,
she said, as my father had died, because all
of these lands of ours were angered. No one
remembered the simple beauty of a clear dawn
and how snow fell covering the streets
littered with lies. Toward dawn she rose
and watched the light graying the still waters
and held me to the window and bobbed me up
and down until I awakened a moment to
see the golden sun splashed upon the eye

of the world. You wonder why I am
impossible, why I stand in the bus station
in Toledo baying No! No! and hurling
the luggage of strangers every which way,
why I refuse to climb ladders or descend into
cellars of coal dust and dead mice or eat
like a good boy or change my dirty clothes
no matter who complains. Look in my eyes!
They have stared into the burning eyes of earth,
molten metals, the first sun, a woman's face,
they have seen the snow covering it all
and a new day breaking over the mother sea.
I breathed the truth. I was born in Lucerne.

The Fox

I think I must have lived
once before, not as a man or woman
but as a small, quick fox pursued
through fields of grass and grain
by ladies and gentlemen on horseback.
This would explain my nose
and the small dark tufts of hair
that rise from the base of my spine.
It would explain why I am
so seldom invited out to dinner
and when I am I am never
invited back. It would explain
my loathing for those on horseback
in Central Park and how I can
so easily curse them and challenge
the men to fight and why no matter
how big they are or how young
they refuse to dismount,
for at such times, rock in hand,
I must seem demented.
My anger is sudden and total,
for I am a man to whom anger
usually comes slowly, spreading
like a fever along my shoulders
and back and turning my stomach
to a stone, but this fox anger
is lyrical and complete, as I stand
in the pathway shouting and refusing
to budge, feeling the dignity
of the small creature menaced
by the many and larger. Yes,
I must have been that unseen fox
whose breath sears the thick bushes
and whose eyes burn like opals
in the darkness, who humps
and shits gleefully in the horsepath
softened by moonlight and goes on
feeling the steady measured beat
of his fox heart like a wordless
delicate song, and the quick forepaws
choosing the way unerringly
and the thick furred body following
while the tail flows upward,

68

too beautiful a plume for anyone
except a creature who must proclaim
not ever ever ever
to mounted ladies and their gentlemen.

To Cipriano, in the Wind

Where did your words go,
Cipriano, spoken to me 38 years
ago in the back of Peerless Cleaners,
where raised on a little wooden platform
you bowed to the hissing press
and under the glaring bulb the scars
across your shoulders – 'a gift
of my country' – gleamed like old wood.
'*Dignidad*,' you said into my boy's
wide eyes, 'without is no riches.'
And Ferrente, the dapper Sicilian
coatmaker, laughed. What could
a pants presser know of dignity?
That was the winter of '41, it
would take my brother off to war,
where you had come from, it would
bring great snowfalls, graying
in the streets, and the news of death
racing through the halls of my school.
I was growing. Soon I would be
your height, and you'd tell me
eye to eye, 'Some day the world
is ours, some day you will see.'
And your eyes burned in your fine
white face until I thought you
would burn. That was the winter
of '41, Bataan would fall
to the Japanese and Sam Baghosian
would make the long march
with bayonet wounds in both legs,
and somehow in spite of burning acids
splashed across his chest and the acids
of his own anger rising toward his heart
he would return to us and eat
the stale bread of victory. Cipriano,
do you remember what followed
the worst snow? It rained all night
and in the dawn the streets gleamed,
and within a week wild phlox leaped
in the open fields. I told you
our word for it, 'Spring', and you said,
'Spring, spring, it always come after.'
Soon the Germans rolled east

into Russia and my cousins died. I
walked alone in the warm spring winds
of evening and said, 'Dignity.' I said
your words, Cipriano, into the winds.
I said, 'Someday this will all be ours.'
Come back, Cipriano Mera, step
out of the wind and dressed in the robe
of your pain tell me again that this
world will be ours. Enter my dreams
or my life, Cipriano, come back
out of the wind.

Belief

No one believes in the calm
of the North Wind after a time
of rage and depression.
No one believes the sea cares nothing
for the shore or that
the long black volcanic reefs
that rise and fall from sight
each day are the hands
of some forgotten creature
trying to touch the unknowable
heart of water. No one believes
that the lost breath of a man
who died in 1821 is my breath
and that I will live until
I no longer want to, and then
I will write my name
in water, as he did, and pass
this breath to anyone who can
believe that life comes back
again and again without end
and always with the same face –
the face that broke in daylight
before the waves at Depot Bay
curling shoreward over and over
just after dawn as the sky cracked
into long slender fingers of light
and I heard your breath beside me
calm and sweet as you returned
to the dark crowded harbor of sleep.
That man will never return. He ate
the earth and the creatures of the sea
and the air, and so it is time he fed
the small tough patches of grass
that fight for water and air
between the blocks on the long walk
to and from school, it is time
that whatever he said began
first to echo and then fade
in the mind of no one
who listened, and that the bed
that moaned under his weight
be released, and that his shoes curl
upward at last and die, for they too

were only the skins of other animals,
not the bear or tiger he prayed to be
before he knew he too was animal,
but the slow ox that sheds his flesh
so that we might grow to our full height –
the beasts no one yearns to become
as young men dream of the sudden fox
threading his way up the thick hillside
and the old of the full-bellied seal,
whiskered and wisely playful. At the beach
at Castelldefels in 1965 a stout man
in his bare socks stood
above two young women stretched out
and dressed in almost nothing.
In one hand he held his vest,
his shoes, and his suit jacket
and with the other he pointed to those
portions of them he most admired,
and he named them in the formal,
guttural Spanish of the Catalan gentleman.
He went away with specks of fine sand
caught on his socks to remind him
that to enter the fire is to be burned
and that the finger he pointed would
blacken in time and probe the still earth,
root-like, stubborn, and find its life
in darkness. No one believes he
knew all this and dared the sea
to rise that moment and take him
away on a journey without end
or that the bodies of the drowned collect
light from the farthest stars and rise
at night to glow without song.
No one believes that to die
is beautiful, that after the hard pain
of the last unsaid word I am swept
in a calm out from shore
and hang in the silence of millions
for the first time among all my family
and that the magic of water
which has filled me becomes me
and I flow into every crack and crevice
where light can enter. Even my oak
takes me to heart. I shadow the yard
where you come in the evening
to talk while the light rises slowly

skyward, and you shiver a moment
before you go in, not believing
my voice in your ear and that the tall trees
blowing in the wind are sea sounds.
No one believes that tonight is the journey
across dark water to the lost continent
no one named. Do you hear the wind
rising all around you? That comes
only after this certain joy. Do you hear
the waves breaking, even in the darkness,
radiant and full? Close your eyes, close
them and follow us toward the first light.

Rain Downriver

It has been raining now since
long before dawn, and the windows
of the Arab coffee house of Delray
are steamed over and no one looks
in or out. If I were on my way
home from the great chemical plant
on a bus of sodden men, heads rolling
with each swerve or lurch, I would get
off just here by the pale pink temple
and walk slowly the one block back
and swing open the doors on blue smoke
and that blurred language in which two
plus two means the waters of earth
have no end or beginning. I would sit
down at an empty table and open
a newspaper in which the atoms
of each meaningless lie are weighed
and I would order one bitter cup
and formally salute the ceiling,
which is blue like heaven but is
coming down in long bandages
revealing the wounds of the last rain.
In this state, which is not madness
but Michigan, here in the suburbs
of the City of God, rain brings back
the gasoline we blew in the face
of creation and sulphur which will not
soften iron or even yellow rice.
If the Messenger entered now
and called out, You are my people!
the tired waiter would waken and bring
him a coffee and an old newspaper
so that he might read in the wrong words
why the earth gives each of us
a new morning to begin the day
and later brings darkness to hide
what we did with it. Rain in winter
began first in the mind of God
as only the smallest thought,
but as the years passed quietly
into each other leaving only
the charred remains of empty hands
and the one glass that never overflowed

it came closer like the cold breath
of someone who has run through snow
to bring you news of a first birth
or to give you his abrupt, wet blessing
on the forehead. So now I go back
out into it. From a sky I can
no longer see, the fall of evening
glistens around my shoulders that
also glisten, and the world is mine.

The Suit

Dark brown pinstripe, the trousers
rising almost to my armpits
and descending, pleated, to great
bellows at the knees, only to close
down just above my shoes. This
was my fine suit, made of God
knows what hard fiber that would
not give or crease. And such
shoulders as no one my height
and under 150 pounds has ever had,
and the great wide swooning lapel
of the double-breasted job buttoning
just below the crotch. So robed, I
was officially dubbed a punk or wild
motherfucker depending on the streets
I glided down. Three times I wore it
formally: first with red suspenders
to a high school dance where no one
danced except the chaperones, in a style
that minimised the fear of gonorrhea.
It was so dark no one recognised me,
and I went home, head down. Then to a party
to which almost no one came and those
who did counted the minutes until
the birthday cake with its armored
frosting was cut and we could flee.
And finally to the draft board where
I stuffed it in a basket with my shoes,
shirt, socks, and underclothes and was
herded naked with the others past doctors
half asleep and determined to find
nothing. That long day it cracked
from indifference or abuse, and so I wore it
on the night shift at Detroit Transmission
where day after day it grew darker and more
unrecognisably tattered like all my
other hopes for a singular life in a rich
world that would be of certain design:
just, proportioned, equal and different
for each of us and satisfying like that flush
of warmth that came with knowing
no one could be more ridiculous than I.

On My Own

Yes, I only got here on my own.
Nothing miraculous. An old woman
opened her door expecting the milk,
and there I was, seven years old, with
a bulging suitcase of wet cardboard
and my hair plastered down and stiff
in the cold. She didn't say, 'Come in',
she didn't say anything. Her luck
had always been bad, so she stood
to one side and let me pass, trailing
the unmistakable aroma of badger
which she mistook for my underwear,
and so she looked upward, not
to heaven but to the cracked ceiling
her husband had promised to mend,
and she sighed for the first time
in my life that sigh which would tell
me what was for dinner. I found my room
and spread my things on the sagging bed:
the bright ties and candy-striped shirts,
the knife to cut bread, the stuffed weasel
to guard the window, the silver spoon
to turn my tea, the pack of cigarettes
for the life ahead, and at last
the little collection of worn-out books
from which I would choose my only name –
Morgan the Pirate, Jack Dempsey, the Prince
of Wales. I chose Abraham Plain
and went off to school wearing a cap
that said 'Ford' in the right script.
The teachers were soft-spoken women
smelling like washed babies and the students
fierce as lost dogs, but they all hushed
in wonder when I named the 400 angels
of death, the planets sighted and unsighted,
the moment at which creation would turn
to burned feathers and blow every which way
in the winds of shock. I sat down
and the room grew quiet and warm. My eyes
asked me to close them. I did, and so
I discovered the beauty of sleep and that
to get ahead I need only say I was there,
and everything would open as the darkness

in my silent head opened onto seascapes
at the other end of the world, waves
breaking into mountains of froth, the sand
running back to become the salt savor
of the infinite. Mrs Tarbox woke me
for lunch – a tiny container of milk
and chocolate cookies in the shape of Michigan.
Of course I went home at 3:30, with
the bells ringing behind me and four stars
in my notebook and drinking companions
on each arm. If you had been there
in your yellow harness and bright hat
directing traffic you would never
have noticed me – my clothes shabby
and my eyes bright –; to you I'd have been
just an ordinary kid. Sure, now you
know, now it's obvious, what with the light
of the Lord streaming through the nine
windows of my soul and the music of rain
following in my wake and the ordinary air
on fire every blessed day I waken the world.

from **SWEET WILL** (1985)

Salts and Oils

In Havana in 1948 I ate fried dog
believing it was Peking duck. Later,
in Tampa I bunked with an insane sailor
who kept a .38 Smith and Wesson in his shorts.
In the same room were twins, oilers
from Toledo, who argued for hours
each night whose turn it was
to get breakfast and should he turn
the eggs or not. On the way north
I lived for three days on warm water
in a DC-6 with a burned out radio
on the runway at Athens, Georgia. We sang
a song, 'Georgia's Big Behind', and prayed
for WWIII and complete, unconditional surrender.
Napping in an open field near Newport News,
I chewed on grass while the shadows of September
lengthened; in the distance a man hammered
on the roof of a hangar and groaned how he
was out of luck and vittles. Bummed a ride
in from Mitchell Field and had beet borscht
and white bread at 34th and 8th Avenue.
I threw up in the alley behind the YMCA
and slept until they turned me out.
I walked the bridge to Brooklyn
while the East River browned below.
A mile from Ebbetts Field, from all
that history, I found Murray, my papa's
buddy, in his greasy truck shop, polishing
replacement parts. Short, unshaven, puffed,
he strutted the filthy aisles,
a tiny Genghis Khan. He sent out for soup
and sandwiches. The world turned on barley,
pickled meats, yellow mustard, kasha,
rye breads. It rained in October, rained
so hard I couldn't walk and smoke, so I
chewed pepsin chewing-gum. The rain
spoiled Armistice Day in Lancaster, Pa.
The open cars overflowed, girls cried,
the tubas and trombones went dumb,

the floral displays shredded, the gutters
clogged with petals. Afterwards had ham
on buttered whole-wheat bread, ham
and butter for the first time
on the same day in Zanesville with snow
forecast, snow, high winds, closed roads,
solid darkness before 5 P.M. These were not
the labors of Hercules, these were not
of meat or moment to anyone but me
or destined for story or to learn from
or to make me fit to take the hand
of a toad or a toad princess or to stand
in line for food stamps. One quiet morning
at the end of my thirteenth year a little bird
with a dark head and tattered tail feathers
had come to the bedroom window and commanded
me to pass through the winding miles
of narrow dark corridors and passageways
of my growing body the filth and glory
of the palatable world. Since then I've
been going out and coming back
the way a swallow does with unerring grace
and foreknowledge because all of this
was prophesied in the final, unread book
of the Midrash and because I have to
grow up and because it pleases me.

Look

The low-built houses of the poor
were all around him, and it
was dawn now, and he was more
awake than not. So it is
a young man begins his life.
Someone, probably his brother,
has quietly closed the front
door, and he feels a sudden gust
of cold air and opens his eyes.
Through the uncurtained window
the great factory sulks in gray
light, there where his mother
must be finishing the night,
her arms crossed and immersed
in the deep, milky washbasin,
those long and slender arms
that seem to him as hard
and drawn as a man's, and
now she would be smiling
with one eye closed and blurred
by the first cigarette in hours.
He sits up and lights his first
too and draws the smoke in
as deeply as he can and feels
his long nakedness stretched
out before him, filling the bed
now grown too small for him.
They will pass, mother and son,
on the street, and he will hold
her straight, taut body for
a moment and smell the grease
in her hair and touch her lips
with his, and today he will not
wonder why the tears start and
stall in her eyes and in his.
Today for the first time in
his life he will let his hands
stray across her padded back
and shoulders, feeling them
give and then hold, and he will
not say one word, not *mother*
or *Ruth* or *goodbye*. If you
are awake in the poor light

of this November, have a look
down at the street that leads
the way you too will have soon
to take. Do you see them there
stopped in each others' arms,
these two who love each other?
Go ahead and look! You wanted
to live as much as they did,
you asked the day to start,
and the day started, but not
because you asked. Forward
or back, they've got no place
to go. No one's blaming you.

Sweet Will

The man who stood beside me
34 years ago this night fell
on to the concrete, oily floor
of Detroit Transmission, and we
stepped carefully over him until
he wakened and went back to his press.

It was Friday night, and the others
told me that every Friday he drank
more than he could hold and fell
and he wasn't any dumber for it
so just let him get up at his
own sweet will or he'll hit you.

'At his own sweet will', was just
what the old black man said to me,
and he smiled the smile of one
who is still surprised that dawn
graying the cracked and broken windows
could start us all to singing in the cold.

Stash rose and wiped the back of his head
with a crumpled handkerchief and looked
at his own blood as though it were
dirt and puzzled as to how
it got there and then wiped the ends
of his fingers carefully one at a time

the way the mother wipes the fingers
of a sleeping child, and climbed back
on his wooden soda-pop case to
his punch press and hollered at all
of us over the oceanic roar of work,
addressing us by our names and nations –

'Nigger, Kike, Hunky, River Rat',
but he gave it a tune, an old tune,
like 'America the Beautiful'. And he danced
a little two-step and smiled showing
the four stained teeth left in the front
and took another suck of cherry brandy.

In truth it was no longer Friday,
for night had turned to day as it
often does for those who are patient,
so it was Saturday in the year of '48
in the very heart of the city of man
where your Cadillac cars get manufactured.

In truth all those people are dead,
they have gone up to heaven singing
'Time on My Hands' or 'Begin the Beguine',
and the Cadillacs have all gone back
to earth, and nothing that we made
that night is worth more than me.

And in truth I'm not worth a thing
what with my feet and my two bad eyes
and my one long nose and my breath
of old lies and my sad tales of men
who let the earth break them back,
each one, to dirty blood or bloody dirt.

Not worth a thing! Just like it was said
at my magic birth when the stars
collided and fire fell from great space
into great space, and people rose one
by one from cold beds to tend a world
that runs on and on at its own sweet will.

An Ordinary Morning

A man is singing on the bus
coming in from Toledo.
His voice floats over the heads
that bow and sway with each
turn, jolt, and sudden slowing.
A hoarse, quiet voice, it tells
of love that is true, of love
that endures a whole weekend.
The driver answers in a tenor
frayed from cigarettes, coffee,
and original curses thrown
down from his seat of command.
He answers that he has time
on his hands and it's heavy.
O heavy hangs the head, he
improvises, and the man
back in the very last row,
bouncing now on the cobbles
as we bump down the boulevard,
affirms that it is hanging,
yes, and that it is heavy.
This is what I waken to.
One by one my near neighbors
open their watering eyes
and close their mouths to accept
this bright, sung conversation
on the theme of their morning.
The sun enters from a cloud
and shatters the wide windshield
into seventeen distinct shades
of yellow and fire, the brakes
gasp and take hold, and we are
the living, newly arrived
in Detroit, city of dreams,
each on his own black throne.

from **A WALK WITH TOM JEFFERSON** (1988)

Buying and Selling

All the way across the Bay Bridge I sang
to the cool winds buffeting my Ford,
for I was on my way to a life of buying
untouched drive shafts, universal joints,
perfect bearings so steeped in Cosmoline
they could endure a century and still retain
their purity of functional design, they
could outlast everything until like us
their usefulness became legend and they
were transformed into sculpture. At Benicia
or the Oakland Naval Yard or Alameda
I left the brilliant Western sun behind
to enter the wilderness of warehouses
with one sullen enlisted man as guide.
There under the blinking artificial light
I was allowed to unwrap a single sample,
to hack or saw my way with delicacy
through layer after layer of cardboard,
metallic paper, cloth webbing, wax
as hard as wood until the dulled steel
was revealed beneath. I read, if I could,
the maker's name, letters, numbers,
all of which translated into functions
and values known only to the old moguls
of the great international junk companies
of Chicago, Philadelphia, Brooklyn,
whose young emissary I was. I, who at
twenty had wept publicly in the Dexter-
Davison branch of the public library
over the death of Keats in the Colvin
biography and had prayed like him
to be among the immortals, now lived
at thirty by a code of figures so arcane
they passed from one side of the brain
to the other only in darkness. I, who
at twenty-six had abandoned several careers
in salesmanship – copper kitchenware,
Fuller brushes, American encyclopedias –
from door to unanswered door in the down

87

and out neighborhoods of Detroit, turning
in my sample cases like a general handing
over his side arms and swagger stick, I
now relayed the new gospels across mountains
and the Great Plains states to my waiting masters.
The news came back: Bid! And we did
and did so in secret. The bids were
awarded, so trucks were dispatched,
Mohawks, Tam O'Shanters, Iroquois.
In new Wellingtons, I stood to one side
while the fork lifts did their work,
entering only at the final moment to pay
both loaders and drivers their pittances
not to steal, to buy at last what could
not be bought. The day was closing down.
Even in California the afternoon skies
must turn from blue to a darker blue
and finally take the color of coal, and stars
– the same or similar ones – hidden so long
above the Chicago River or the IRT
to Brooklyn, emerge stubbornly not in ones
but in pairs, for there is safety in numbers.
Silent, alone, I would stand in the truck's
gray wake feeling something had passed,
was over, complete. The great metal doors
of the loading dock crashed down, and in
the sudden aftermath I inhaled a sadness
stronger than my Lucky Strike, stronger
than the sadness of these hills and valleys
with their secret ponds and streams unknown
even to children, or the sadness of children
themselves, who having been abandoned believe
their parents will return before dark.

At 28 I was still faithless.
I had crossed the country in a green Ford,
sleeping one night almost 14 hours in a motel
above Salt Lake City. I discovered
I'd had a fever all that day and thus the animals
that dotted the road, the small black spots
that formed and unformed crows, the flying pieces
of slate that threatened to break through
the windshield…were whatever they were.
I took two aspirins and an allergy pill – that was all
I had – and got into bed although it was light out.
That was 28 years ago. Since then I have died
only twice, once in slow motion against
the steel blue driver's side of a Plymouth
station wagon. One moment before impact I said
to myself, seriously, 'This is going to hurt.'
The kids in the Plymouth's back seat gaped
wildly, shouted, leaped, and the father held firm
to the steering wheel as I slipped through the space
that was theirs, untouched, skidding first
on the black field of asphalt and broken glass
that is California 168, Tollhouse Road, and over
the edge of the mountain, the motorcycle
tumbling off on its own through nettles and grass
to come to a broken rest as all bodies must.
Often when I shave before a late dinner, especially
on summer evenings, I notice the white lines
on my right shoulder like the smeared imprint
of a leaf on silk or the delicate tracings
on a whale's fins that the smaller sea animals carve
to test his virtue, and I re-enter the wide blue eyes
of that family of five that passed on their way
up the mountain.
                    But at 28 I was still faithless.
I could rise before dawn from a bed drenched
with my own sweat, repack the green Ford
in the dark, my own breath steaming
in the high, clear air, and head for California.
I could spend the next night in Squaw Valley
writing a letter to my wife and kids asleep hours
behind me in Colorado, I could listen to Rexroth
reminiscing on a Berkeley FM station in the voice
God uses to lecture Jesus Christ and still believe

two aspirins, an allergy pill, and proper rest were proof
against the cold that leaps in one blind moment
from the heart to the farthest shore to shudder
through the small sea creatures I never knew existed.

It seems the sun passing back and forth behind clouds
this morning threatens to withdraw its affections
and the sky is as distant and pale as a bored child
in the wrong classroom or a man of 28
drilled so often on the names of fruit-bearing trees
that he forgets even the date palm. Here in New England,
no longer new or English, the first frost
has stained the elms and maples outside my window,
and the kids on their way hunch their shoulders
against the cold. One boy drops his lunch-box
with a clatter and mysteriously leaves it there
on the pavement as a subtle rebuke
to his mother, to a father holding tight to a wheel,
to a blue Plymouth that long ago entered the heaven
brooding above Detroit. If only they had stopped
all those years ago and become a family of five
descending one after the other the stone ledges
of Sweet Potato Mountain and found me face down
among the thistles and shale and lifted me to my feet.
I weighed no more than feathers do or the wish
to become pure spirit. If I had not broken my glasses
I could have gone on my way with a thank you,
with a gap-toothed smile.   28 years ago, faithless, I
found the great bay of San Francisco where the map
said it would be and crossed the bridge from Oakland
singing 'I Cover the Waterfront' into the cold winds
and the dense odor of coffee. Before I settled
in East Palo Alto among divorcees and appliance salesmen,
fifty yards from the Union Pacific tracks, I spent a long weekend
with Arthur, my mentor to be. In a voice ruined, he said,
by all-night draughts of whiskey and coffee, he praised
the nobility of his lemon and orange trees, the tang
of his loquats, the archaic power of his figs.
In a gambler's green visor and stiff Levis, he bowed
to his wounded tomatoes swelling into late summer.
Kneeling in the parched loam by the high fence
he bared the elusive strawberries, his blunt fingers
working the stiff leaves over and over. It was August.
He was almost happy.
                   Faithless, I had not found

the olive trees bursting on the hillsides west
of US 99. I knew only the bitter black fruit
that clings with all its life to the hard seed.
I had not wakened to mockers wrangling in my yard
at dawn in a riot of sexual splendor or heard
the sea roar at Bondy Bay, the long fingers
of ocean running underneath the house all night
to rinse off the pain of nightmare. I had not
seen my final child, though he was on the way.
I had not become a family of five nor opened
my arms to receive the black gifts of a mountain road,
of ground cinders, pebbles, rough grass.

                            At twice my age
Arthur, too, was faithless, or so he insisted
through the long sober evenings in Los Altos, once
crowded with the cries of coyotes. His face
darkened and his fists shook when he spoke
of Nothing, what he would become in that waiting blaze
of final cold, a whiteness like no other.
At 56, more scared of me than I of him,
his right forefinger raised to keep the beat,
he gravelled out his two great gifts of truth:
'I'd rather die than reread the last novels
of Henry James,' and, 'Philip, we must never lie
or we shall lose our souls.' All one winter afternoon
he chanted in Breton French the coarse poems of Tristan Corbière,
his voice reaching into unforeseen sweetness, both hands
rising toward the ceiling, the tears held back so long
still held back, for he was dying and he was ready.

By April I had crossed the Pacheco Pass and found
roosting in the dark branches of the Joshua tree
the fabled magpie – 'Had a long tongue and a long tail;
He could both talk and do.' This is a holy land,
I thought. At a Sonoco station the attendant,
wiry and dour, said in perfect Okie, 'Be careful, son,
a whole family was wiped out right here
just yesterday.' At Berenda the fields flooded
for miles in every direction. Arthur's blank sky
stared down at an unruffled inland sea and threatened
to let go. On the way home I cut lilacs
from the divider strip of El Camino Real.
My wife was pregnant. All night we hugged
each other in our narrow bed as the rain
came on in sheets. A family of five, and all
of us were out of work. The dawn was silent.

The black roses, battered, unclenched, the burned petals
floated on the pond beside the playhouse.
Beneath the surface the tiny stunned pike circled
no prey we could see. That was not another life.
I was 29 now and faithless, not the father of the man
I am but the same man who all this day
sat in a still house watching the low clouds massing
in the west, the new winds coming on.
By late afternoon the kids are home from school,
clambering on my front porch, though day
after day I beg them not to. When I go
to the window they race off in mock horror,
daring me to follow. The huge crows that wake
me every morning settle back on the rain spout
next door to caw to the season. I could put them
all in a poem, title it 'The Basket of Memory'
as though each image were an Easter egg waiting to hatch
as though I understood the present and the past
or even why the 8 year old with a cap of blond hair
falling to her shoulders waves to me as she darts
between parked cars and cartwheels into the early dusk.

A Theory of Prosody

When Nellie, my old pussy
cat, was still in her prime,
she would sit behind me
as I wrote, and when the line
got too long she'd reach
one sudden black foreleg down
and paw at the moving hand,
the offensive one. The first
time she drew blood I learned
it was poetic to end
a line anywhere to keep her
quiet. After all, many morn-
ings she'd gotten to the chair
long before I was even up.
Those nights I couldn't sleep
she'd come and sit in my lap
to calm me. So I figured
I owed her the short cat line.
She's dead now almost nine years,
and before that there was one
during which she faked attention
and I faked obedience.
Isn't that what it's about –
pretending there's an alert cat
who leaves nothing to chance.

A Walk with Tom Jefferson

Between the freeway
                and the gray conning towers
of the ballpark, miles
                of mostly vacant lots, once
a neighborhood of small
                two-storey wooden houses –
dwellings for immigrants
                from Ireland, Germany,
Poland, West Virginia,
                Mexico, Dodge Main.
A little world with only
                three seasons, or so we said –
one to get tired, one to get
                old, one to die.
No one puts in irises,
                and yet before March passes
the hard green blades push
                their way through
where firm lawns once were.
                The trunks of beech and locust
darken, the light new branches
                take the air. You can
smell the sticky sap rising
                in the maples, smell it
even over the wet stink
                of burned houses.
On this block seven houses
                are still here to be counted,
and if you count the shacks
                housing illegal chickens,
the pens for dogs, the tiny
                pig sty that is half cave…
and if you count them you can
                count the crows' nest
in the high beech tree
                at the corner, and you can
regard the beech tree itself
                bronzing in mid-morning light
as the mast of the great ship
                sailing us all back
into the 16th century
                or into the present age's
final discovery. (Better
                perhaps not to speak

of final anything, for
                    this place was *finally* retired,
the books thrown away
                    when after the town exploded
in '67 these houses
                    were plundered for whatever
they had. Some burned
                    to the ground, some
hung open, doorless, wide-eyed
                    until hauled off
by the otherwise unemployable
                    citizens of the county
to make room for the triumphant
                    return of Mad Anthony Wayne,
Père Marquette, Cadillac,
                    the badger, the wolverine,
the meadow lark, the benign
                    long toothed bi-ped
with nothing on his mind.)
                    During baseball season
the neighborhood's a thriving
                    business for anyone
who can make change
                    and a cardboard sign
that reads 'Parking $3'.
                    He can stand on the curb
directing traffic and pretending
                    the land is his.
On August nights I come
                    out here after ten
and watch the light rise
                    from the great gray bowl
of the stadium, watch it catch
                    a scrap of candy wrapper
in the wind, a soiled napkin
                    or a peanut shell and turn
it into fire or the sound
                    of fire as the whole world
holds its breath. In the last
                    inning 50,000
pulling at the night
                    air for one last scream.
They can drain the stars
                    of light. No one
owns any of this.
                    It's condemned,

but the money for the execution
            ran out years ago.
Money is a dream, part
            of the lost past.
Joe Louis grew up a few miles
            east of here and attended
Bishop Elementary.
            No one recalls
a slender, dumbfounded
            boy afraid of his fifth grade
home room teacher. Tom Jefferson
            – 'Same name as the other one' –
remembers Joe at seventeen
            all one sweltering summer
unloading bales of rags
            effortlessly from the trucks
that parked in the alley
            behind Wolfe Sanitary Wiping Cloth.
'Joe was beautiful,'
            is all he says, and we two
go dumb replaying Joe's
            glide across the ring
as he corners Schmeling
            and prepares to win
World War II. Like Joe
            Tom was up from Alabama,
like Joe he didn't talk
            much then, and even now
he passes a hand across
            his mouth when speaking
of the $5 day that lured
            his father from the cotton fields
and a one-room shack the old folks
            talked about until
they went home first
            to visit and later to die.
Early afternoon behind
            his place, Tom's gathering up
the remnants of this year's
            garden – the burned
tomato plants and the hardy
            runners of summer squash
that dug into the chalky
            soil and won't let go.
He stuffs the dried remains
            into a supermarket shopping cart

to haul off to an empty block.
               The zinnias are left,
the asters in browns and dirty
               yellows, tough petalled
autumn blooms, even a few
               sticky green rose buds
climbing a telephone pole.
               Alabama is not so far back
it's lost in a swirl
               of memory. 'I can see trees
behind the house. I do
               believe I still feel
winter mornings, all of us
               getting up from one bed
but for what I don't know.'
               He tips his baseball cap
to the white ladies passing
               back the way we've come.
'We all come for $5
               a day and we got this!'
His arms spread wide to
               include block after block
of dumping grounds,
               old couches and settees
burst open, the white innards
               gone gray, cracked
and mangled chifforobes
               that long ago gave up
their secrets, yellow wooden
               ice boxes yawning
at the sky, their breath
               still fouled with years
of eating garlic sausage
               and refried beans,
the shattered rib cages
               of beds that couldn't hold
our ordinary serviceable dreams,
               blue mattresses stained
in earnest, the cracked
               toilet seats of genius,
whole market counters
               that once contained the red meats
we couldn't get enough of,
               burned out electric motors,
air conditioners
               we suffocated, and over all

an arctic wind from Canada
                which carries off
the final faint unseeable
                spasm of the desire
to be human and brings down
                the maple and elm leaves
of early October. If you follow
                their trail of burnished arrows
scuttling across curbs and cracked
                sidewalks they'll lead
you to the cellar hole
                of something or someone
called Dogman. 'Making do,'
                says Tom Jefferson.
His neighbors swear
                someone runs on all fours
with his dog packs. They claim
                they can tell when
their own dogs feel the pull
                of the wild ones.
The women talk of lost
                house cats grown to the size
of cougars. They've heard them
                crashing through the dense
underbrush of the dumping
                ground and found
huge paw tracks in the snow,
                the remains of drunks
and children caught out
                after dark, nothing but clean bones
revealed under ice when
                the spring rains come back.
'There ain't no kids
                around here,' says Tom,
'But if there were, the bones
                be about the same size.'
Tom has seen vapor rising
                through the missing floorboards,
clouds of it, and maybe
                animals and man
together producing a new
                variety of steam heat.
Even I have seen a brutish
                black mongrel Dane
in late afternoon, his coat
                snow flecked, rising

on his hind legs to over
          seven feet, hanging
over fences, peering in windows
          as though he yearned
to come back to what
          we were. Winter's in everything
we say – it's coming on – we see
          it in the mad swirl
of leaves and newspapers
          doing their dances.
We feel it as iron
          in the wind. We could escape,
each of us feels in
          his shuddering heart, take
the bridge south to Canada,
          but we don't. Instead we
hunker down, slump a little
          lower in our trousers,
and go slow. One night soon
          I'll waken to a late quiet
and go out to see all this
          transformed, each junked car,
each dumping ground and battered
          hovel a hill
of mounded snow, every scrap
          of ugliness redeemed
under the light of a street lamp
          or the moon. From the dark tower
of the Renaissance Center Ford built
          to look down
on our degradation to the great
          Ford plant downriver blowing
its black breath in the face
          of creation, the one at Rouge
where he broke first our backs
          and then the rest, everything
silent, suspended in a new world
          like no other. For a moment
a few stars come out to share
          this witness. I won't believe it,
but Tom will. Tom Jefferson
          is a believer.
You can't plant winter vegetables
          if you aren't,
you can't plant anything, except
          maybe radishes.

You don't have to believe
                anything to grow
radishes. Early August he's got
                sweet corn
two feet above his head,
                he stretches
his arm to show where
                they grow to.
Tomatoes 'remind you what tomatoes
                taste like'.
He was planting before the Victory Gardens.
                His mother brought
the habit up from Alabama. She was
                growing greens
behind the house no matter how small
                her strip of land,
cosmos beside the back door,
                early things
like pansies along the fence.
                'Why she could go
into a bare field and find
                the purple flags,
wild, bring them home, half-
                dead dirty chicks
on the palm of her hand, and they'd
                grow. I could
never do that, I gave up trying
                fifty years ago.'
It didn't take FDR
                and 'the war effort'
to make a believer out of Tom.
                When he went off to war
his son Tom Jr took over
                the garden and did
a job, the same son went off
                to Korea and didn't
come home, the son he seldom talks
                about, just as he
seldom talks about his three years
                in the Seabees
building airstrips so we could
                bomb Japan, doing
the war work he did at home
                for less pay.
A father puts down a spade, his son
                picks it up,

'That's Biblical,' he says,
        'the son goes off,
the father takes up the spade
        again, that's Biblical.'
He'd leave for work in the cold
        dark of December.
Later, out the high broken windows
        at Dodge Main
he'd see the snow falling
        silently and know
it was falling on the dark petals
        of the last rose,
know his wife was out
        back hunched
in her heavy gray sweater
        letting those first flakes
slowly settle into
        water on the warm
red flesh of the dime store
        plants Tom Jr
put in on his own.
        Later he'd come home
in the early dark
        with snow on his hair,
tracking the dirty
        snow on her rug –
they say the dogs yellow
        it before it hits
the ground – and she would
        say nothing.
'That's Biblical,' he says.
        'We couldn't even look
near each other
        for fear of how
one might make the other cry.
        That's Biblical,
knowing the other so well
        you know yourself,
being careful the way she was
        never to say nothing
or show the least sign.'
        Tom picks a maple leaf
stiff backed and brown
        from the gutter,
holds it against the distant
        pale sky streaked

with contrails. Maybe even
       war is Biblical, maybe
even the poor white
       fighting the poor black
in this city for the same
       gray concrete housing,
the same gray jobs
       they both came
north for, maybe that's
       Biblical, the way
the Canaanites and the Philistines
       fought the Israelites,
and the Israelites killed
       the Amalakites
always for the same land.
       'God wanted Saul
to kill them down to the last lamb.
       He didn't,
and he went crazy. Back
       in the riots of '42
they did not kill us down
       to the last lamb.
They needed us making airfields
       the way they needed us
making Fords before the war,
       maybe that's why
they went crazy.' There at the end
       of the street is his house,
his since he came home
       and could never leave.
The wisteria along the side
       has grown to the thicknes
of his own wrist, the back yard
       is roses still, squash
coming on, onions in late
       bloom to be tricked
by the first cold, potatoes
       hidden underground,
they think, forever.
       'It's Biblical.
The way David plays for Saul so he
       can weep, and later
when his turn comes David
       weeps for Absalom.
It's Biblical, you cry,
       it's Biblical you don't,

either way. That's Biblical.'
                What commandment
was broken to bring God's
                wrath down on these streets,
what did we wrong, going
                about our daily lives,
to work at all hours until
                the work dried up,
then sitting home until home
                became a curse
with the yellow light
                of afternoon falling
with all the weight of final
                judgement, I can't say.
It's Biblical, this season
                of color coming
to its end, the air swirling
                in tiny cyclones
of brown and red, the air
                swelling my lungs,
banging about my ears so that
                I almost think I hear
Tom say 'Absalom' again, a name
                owed to autumn
and the autumn of his hopes.
                It's Biblical,
the little pyres pluming
                the afternoon gray and blue
on these corners, the calm
                of these childless streets,
a dog howling from a distant
                block, another answering,
the calls of the chained animals
                going back and forth
so plaintive and usual no one
                hears. The sparrows
fan out across the grassless yards
                busily seeking
whatever seeds the cold winds
                burst forth, and this
day is coming to its end
                with only the smallest
winter birds to keep
                the vigil. 'We need
this season,' Tom has said,
                but Tom believes

the roots need cold,
          the earth needs to turn
to ice and snow so a new fire
          can start up in the heart
of all that grows.
          He doesn't say that.
He doesn't say the heart
          of ice is fire waiting,
he doesn't say the new seed
          nestles in the old,
waiting, frozen, for the land
          to thaw, and even these streets
of cracking blacktop long gone gray,
          the seven junked cars
the eye can note collapsed
          on slashed tires, their insides
drawn out for anything, he doesn't
          say all this is a lost land,
it's Biblical. He parks his chromed
          shopping cart under the porch,
brushes the dirt and leaves
          from his worn corduroy –
six feet of man, unbowed –
          and locks the knee-high gate
of his fence that could
          hold back no one,
smiles and says the one word,
          'Tomorrow,' and goes in.
Later he'll put the porch light on,
          though no one's coming.
The crazy Indian colors
          are blooming as the sun
begins to go, deep maroons
          they tell us are the signs
of all the earth we've pumped
          into the sky.
The same rich browns the ground
          reveals after rain,
the veins of orange I've uncovered
          digging the yard
spring after spring. Never once
          have I found the least sign
that this was once the Indian's
          ground, perhaps a holy land,
not a single arrowhead
          or shard, though I

have caught a sudden glint of
                what I didn't know
while turning over dirt I swore
                was never turned before
only to kneel to a bottle cap
                polished down
to anonymity or a wad
                of tinfoil
from an empty pack
                of Luckys, curled
to the shape of whatever
                vanished human hand
tossed it off. We were not
                idle hands. Still a kid
when I worked nights
                on the milling machines
at Cadillac transmission,
                another kid just up
from West Virginia asked me
                what was we making,
and I answered, I'm making
                2.25 an hour,
don't know what you're
                making, and he had
to correct me, gently, what was
                we making out of
this here metal, and I didn't know.
                Whatever it was we
made, we made of earth. Amazing earth.
                amazed perhaps
by all it's given us,
                as amazed as I
who stood one afternoon
                forty years ago
at a railroad crossing
                near Joy Road
as the Sherman tanks passed
                two to a flat-bed car,
on their way to a war,
                their long guns
frowning down identically, they
                passed some twenty minutes
or more while the tracks groaned,
                the trestle snapped
and sighed with so much stubborn
                weight of our going.

Later, in the forge room
        at Chevy, now a man,
still making what I never knew,
        I stood in the silence
of the great presses slamming
        home, the roar of earth
striking the fired earth, the reds
        searing their glowing image
into the eye and brain,
        the oranges and roses
blooming in the mind long
        after, even in sleep.
What were we making out
        of this poor earth good
for so much giving and taking?
        (Beets the size of fists
by the thousands, cabbages
        as big as brains
year after year, whole cribs
        of peppers, great lakes
of sweet corn tumbling
        by the trailer load,
it gave and gave, and whatever
        we had it took.)
The place was called Chevy
        Gear & Axle –
it's gone now, gone to earth
        like so much here –
so perhaps we actually made
        gears and axles
for the millions of Chevies
        long dead or still to die.
It said that, 'Chevrolet
        Gear & Axle'
right on the checks they paid
        us with, so I can
half-believe that's what we
        were making way back then.

Fear and Fame

Half an hour to dress, wide rubber hip boots,
gauntlets to the elbow, a plastic helmet
like a knight's but with a little glass window
that kept steaming over, and a respirator
to save my smoke-stained lungs. I would descend
step by slow step into the dim world
of the pickling tank and there prepare
the new solutions from the great carboys
of acids lowered to me on ropes – all from a recipe
I shared with nobody and learned from Frank O'Mera
before he went off to the bars on Vernor Highway
to drink himself to death. A gallon of hydrochloric
steaming from the wide glass mouth, a dash
of pale nitric to bubble up, sulphuric to calm,
metals for sweeteners, cleansers for salts,
until I knew the burning stew was done.
Then to climb back, step by stately step, the adventurer
returned to the ordinary blinking lights
of the swingshift at Feinberg and Breslin's
First-Rate Plumbing and Plating with a message
from the kingdom of fire. Oddly enough
no one welcomed me back, and I'd stand
fully armored as the downpour of cold water
rained down on me and the smoking traces puddled
at my feet like so much milk and melting snow.
Then to disrobe down to my work pants and shirt,
my black street shoes and white cotton socks,
to reassume my nickname, strap on my Bulova,
screw back my wedding-ring, and with tap water
gargle away the bitterness as best I could.
For fifteen minutes or more I'd sit quietly
off to the side of the world as the women
polished the tubes and fixtures to a burnished purity
hung like Christmas ornaments on the racks
pulled steadily toward the tanks I'd cooked.
Ahead lay the second cigarette, held in a shaking hand,
as I took into myself the sickening heat to quell heat,
a lunch of two Genoa salami sandwiches and Swiss cheese
on heavy peasant bread baked by my Aunt Tsipie,

and a third cigarette to kill the taste of the others.
Then to arise and dress again in the costume
of my trade for the second time that night, stiffened
by the knowledge that to descend and rise up
from the other world merely once in eight hours is half
what it takes to be known among women and men.

Coming Close

Take this quiet woman, she has been
standing before a polishing wheel
for over three hours, and she lacks
twenty minutes before she can take
a lunch break. Is she a woman?
Consider the arms as they press
the long brass tube against the buffer,
they are striated along the triceps,
the three heads of which clearly show.
Consider the fine dusting of dark down
above the upper lip, and the beads
of sweat that run from under the red
kerchief across the brow and are wiped
away with a blackening wrist band
in one odd motion a child might make
to say No! No! You must come closer
to find out, you must hang your tie
and jacket in one of the lockers
in favor of a black smock, you must
be prepared to spend shift after shift
hauling off the metal trays of stock,
bowing first, knees bent for a purchase,
then lifting with a gasp, the first word
of tenderness between the two of you,
then you must bring new trays of dull
unpolished tubes. You must feed her,
as they say in the language of the place.
Make no mistake, the place has a language,
and if by some luck the power were cut,
the wheel slowed to a stop so that you
suddenly saw it was not a solid object
but so many separate bristles forming
in motion a perfect circle, she would turn
to you and say, 'Why?' Not the old *why*
of *why must I spend five nights a week?*
Just, 'Why?' Even if by some magic
you knew, you wouldn't dare speak
for fear of her laughter, which now
you have anyway as she places the five
tapering fingers of her filthy hand
on the arm of your white shirt to mark
you for your own, now and forever.

Every Blessed Day

First with a glass of water
tasting of iron and then
with more and colder water
over his head he gasps himself
awake. He hears the *cheep*
of winter birds searching
the snow for crumbs of garbage
and knows exactly how much light
and how much darkness is there
before the dawn, gray and weak,
slips between the buildings.
Closing the door behind him,
he thinks of places he
has never seen but heard
about, of the great desert
his father said was like
no sea he had ever crossed
and how at dusk or dawn
it held all the shades of red
and blue in its merging shadows,
and though his life was then
a prison he had come to live
for these suspended moments.
Waiting at the corner he feels
the cold at his back and stamps
himself awake again. Seven miles
from the frozen, narrow river.
Even before he looks he knows
the faces on the bus, some
going to work and some coming back,
but each sealed in its hunger
for a different life, a lost life.
Where he's going or who he is
he doesn't ask himself, he
doesn't know and doesn't know
it matters. He gets off
at the familiar corner, crosses
the emptying parking lots
toward Chevy Gear & Axle #3.
In a few minutes he will hold
his time card above a clock,
and he can drop it in
and hear the moment crunching

down, or he can not, for
either way the day will last
forever. So he lets it fall.
If he feels the elusive calm
his father spoke of and searched
for all his short life, there's
no way of telling, for now he's
laughing among them, older men
and kids. He's saying, 'Damn,
we've got it made.' He's
lighting up or chewing with
the others, thousands of miles
from their forgotten homes, each
and every one his father's son.

Among Children

I walk among the rows of bowed heads –
the children are sleeping through fourth grade
so as to be ready for what is ahead,
the monumental boredom of junior high
and the rush forward tearing their wings
loose and turning their eyes forever inward.
These are the children of Flint, their fathers
work at the spark-plug factory or truck
bottled water in 5 gallon sea-blue jugs
to the widows of the suburbs. You can see
already how their backs have thickened,
how their small hands, soiled by pig iron,
leap and stutter even in dreams. I would like
to sit down among them and read slowly
from *The Book of Job* until the windows
pale and the teacher rises out of a milky sea
of industrial scum, her gowns streaming
with light, her foolish words transformed
into song, I would like to arm each one
with a quiver of arrows so that they might
rush like wind there where no battle rages
shouting among the trumpets, Ha! Ha!
How dear the gift of laughter in the face
of the 8 hour day, the cold winter mornings
without coffee and oranges, the long lines
of mothers in old coats waiting silently
where the gates have closed. Ten years ago
I went among these same children, just born,
in the bright ward of the Sacred Heart and leaned
down to hear their breaths delivered that day,
burning with joy. There was such wonder
in their sleep, such purpose in their eyes
closed against autumn, in their damp heads
blurred with the hair of ponds, and not one
turned against me or the light, not one
said, I am sick, I am tired, I will go home,
not one complained or drifted alone,
unloved, on the hardest day of their lives.
Eleven years from now they will become
the men and women of Flint or Paradise,
the majors of a minor town, and I
will be gone into smoke or memory,
so I bow to them here and whisper
all I know, all I will never know.

What Work Is

We stand in the rain in a long line
waiting at Ford Highland Park. For work.
You know what work is – if you're
old enough to read this you know what
work is, although you may not do it.
Forget you. This is about waiting,
shifting from one foot to another.
Feeling the light rain falling like mist
into your hair, blurring your vision
until you think you see your own brother
ahead of you, maybe ten places.
You rub your glasses with your fingers,
and of course it's someone else's brother,
narrower across the shoulders than
yours but with the same sad slouch, the grin
that does not hide the stubbornness,
the sad refusal to give in to
rain, to the hours wasted waiting,
to the knowledge that somewhere ahead
a man is waiting who will say, 'No,
we're not hiring today', for any
reason he wants. You love your brother,
now suddenly you can hardly stand
the love flooding you for your brother,
who's not beside you or behind or
ahead because he's home trying to
sleep off a miserable night shift
at Cadillac so he can get up
before noon to study his German.
Works eight hours a night so he can sing
Wagner, the opera you hate most,
the worst music ever invented.
How long has it been since you told him
you loved him, held his wide shoulders,
opened your eyes wide and said those words,
and maybe kissed his cheek? You've never
done something so simple, so obvious,
not because you're too young or too dumb,
not because you're jealous or even mean
or incapable of crying in
the presence of another man, no,
just because you don't know what work is.

Facts

The bus station in Princeton, New Jersey,
has no men's room. I had to use one like mad,
but the guy behind the counter said, 'Sorry,
but you know what goes on in bus station men's rooms.'

If you take a '37 Packard grill and split it down
the center and reduce the angle by 18° and reweld it,
you'll have a perfect grill for a Rolls Royce
just in case you ever need a new grill for yours.

I was not born in Cleveland, Ohio. Other people
were, or so I have read, and many have remained,
which strikes me as an exercise in futility
greater even than saving your pennies to buy a Rolls.

F. Scott Fitzgerald attended Princeton. A student
pointed out the windows of the suite he occupied.
We were on our way to the train station to escape
to New York City, and the student may have been lying.

The train is called 'The Dinky'. It takes you only
a few miles away to a junction where you can catch
a train to Grand Central or – if you're scared –
to Philadelphia. From either you can reach Cleveland.

My friend Howie wrote me that he was ashamed
to live in a city whose most efficient means of escape
is called 'The Dinky'. If he'd invest in a Rolls,
even one with a Packard grill, he'd feel differently.

I don't blame the student for lying, especially
to a teacher. He may have been ill at ease
in my company, for I am an enormous man given
to long bouts of silence as I brood on facts.

There are two lies in the previous stanza. I'm small,
each year I feel the bulk of me shrinking, becoming
more frail and delicate. I get cold easily as though
I lacked even the solidity to protect my own heart.

The coldest I've ever been was in Cleveland, Ohio.
My host and hostess hated and loved each other
by frantic turns. To escape I'd go on long walks
in the yellowing snow as the evening winds raged.

The citizens of Cleveland, Ohio, passed me sullenly,
benighted in their Rolls Royces, each in a halo
of blue light sifting down from the abandoned
filling stations of what once was a community.

I will never return to Cleveland or Princeton, not
even to pay homage to Hart Crane's lonely tower
or the glory days of John Berryman, whom I loved.
I haven't the heart for it. Not even in your Rolls.

Gin

The first time I drank gin
I thought it must be hair tonic.
My brother swiped the bottle
from a guy whose father owned
a drug store that sold booze
in those ancient, honorable days
when we acknowledged the stuff
was a drug. Three of us passed
the bottle around, each tasting
with disbelief. People paid
for this? People had to have
it, the way we had to have
the women we never got near.
(Actually they were girls, but
never mind, the important fact
was their impenetrability.)
Leo, the third foolish partner,
suggested my brother should have
swiped Canadian whiskey or brandy,
but Eddie defended his choice
on the grounds of the expressions
'gin house' and 'gin lane', both
of which indicated the preeminence
of gin in the world of drinking,
a world we were entering without
understanding how difficult
exit might be. Maybe the bliss
that came with drinking came
only after a certain period
of apprenticeship. Eddie likened
it to the holy man's self-flagellation
to experience the fullness of faith.
(He was very well read for a kid
of fourteen in the public schools.)
So we dug in and passed the bottle
around a second time and then a third,
in the silence each of us expecting
some transformation. 'You get used
to it,' Leo said. 'You don't
like it but you get used to it.'
I know now that brain cells
were dying for no earthly purpose,
that three boys were becoming

increasingly despiritualised
even as they took into themselves
these spirits, but I thought then
I was at last sharing the world
with the movie stars, that before
long I would be shaving because
I needed to, that hair would
sprout across the flat prairie
of my chest and plunge even
to my groin, that first girls
and then women would be drawn
to my qualities. Amazingly, later
some of this took place, but
first the bottle had to be
emptied, and then the three boys
had to empty themselves of all
they had so painfully taken in
and by means even more painful
as they bowed by turns over
the eye of the toilet bowl
to discharge their shame. Ahead
lay cigarettes, the futility
of guaranteed programs of
exercise, the elaborate lies
of conquest no one believed,
forms of sexual torture and
rejection undreamed of. Ahead
lay our fifteenth birthdays,
acne, deodorants, crabs, salves,
butch haircuts, draft registration,
the military and political victories
of Dwight Eisenhower, who brought us
Richard Nixon with wife and dog.
Any wonder we tried gin.

M. Degas Teaches Art & Science at Durfee Intermediate School
Detroit, 1942

He made a line on the blackboard,
one bold stroke from right to left
diagonally downward and stood back
to ask, looking as always at no one
in particular, 'What have I done?'
From the back of the room Freddie
shouted, 'You've broken a piece
of chalk.' M. Degas did not smile.
'What have I done?' he repeated.
The most intellectual students
looked down to study their desks
except for Gertrude Bimmler, who raised
her hand before she spoke. 'M. Degas,
you have created the hypotenuse
of an isosceles triangle.' Degas mused.
Everyone knew that Gertrude could not
be incorrect. 'It is possible,'
Louis Warshowsky added precisely,
'that you have begun to represent
the roof of a barn.' I remember
that it was exactly twenty minutes
past eleven, and I thought at worst
this would go on another forty
minutes. It was early April,
the snow had all but melted on
the playgrounds, the elms and maples
bordering the cracked walks shivered
in the new winds, and I believed
that before I knew it I'd be
swaggering to the candy store
for a Milky Way. M. Degas
pursed his lips, and the room
stilled until the long hand
of the clock moved to twenty-one
as though in complicity with Gertrude,
who added confidently, 'You've begun
to separate the dark from the dark.'
I looked back for help, but now
the trees bucked and quaked, and I
knew this could go on forever.

Soloing

My mother tells me she dreamed
of John Coltrane, a young Trane
playing his music with such joy
and contained energy and rage
she could not hold back her tears.
And sitting awake now, her hands
crossed in her lap, the tears start
in her blind eyes. The TV set
behind her is gray, expressionless.
It is late, the neighbors quiet,
even the city – Los Angeles – quiet.
I have driven for hours down 99,
over the Grapevine into heaven
to be here. I place my left hand
on her shoulder, and she smiles.
What a world, a mother and son
finding solace in California
just where we were told it would
be, among the palm trees and all-
night super markets pushing orange
back-lighted oranges at 2 A.M.
'He was alone,' she says, and does
not say, just as I am, 'soloing.'
What a world, a great man half
her age comes to my mother
in sleep to give her the gift
of song, which – shaking the tears
away – she passes on to me, for now
I can hear the music of the world
in the silence and that word:
soloing. What a world – when I
arrived the great bowl of mountains
was hidden in a cloud of exhaust,
the sea spread out like a carpet
of oil, the roses I had brought
from Fresno browned on the seat
beside me, and I could have
turned back and lost the music.

Scouting

I'm the man who gets off the bus
at the bare junction of nothing
with nothing, and then heads back
to where we've been as though
the future were stashed somewhere
in that tangle of events we call
'Where I come from.' Where I
came from the fences ran right
down to the road, and the lone woman
leaning back on her front porch as she
quietly smoked asked me what did
I want. Confused as always, I
answered, 'Water,' and she came to me
with a frosted bottle and a cup,
shook my hand, and said, 'Good luck.'
That was forty years ago, you say,
when anything was possible. No,
it was yesterday, the gray icebox
sat on the front porch, the crop
was tobacco and not yet in, you
could hear it sighing out back.
The rocker gradually slowed as
she came toward me but never
stopped and the two of us went on
living in time. One of her eyes
had a pale cast and looked nowhere
or into the future where without
regrets she would give up the power
to grant life, and I would darken
like wood left in the rain and then
fade into only a hint of the grain.
I went higher up the mountain
until my breath came in gasps,
my sight darkened, and I slept
to the side of the road to waken
chilled in the sudden July cold,
alone and well. What is it like
to come to, nowhere, in darkness,
not knowing who you are, not
caring if the wind calms, the stars
stall in their sudden orbits,
the cities below go on without
you, screaming and singing?

I don't have the answer. I'm
scouting, getting the feel
of the land, the way the fields
step down the mountainsides
hugging their battered, sagging
wire fences to themselves as though
both day and night they needed
to know their limits. Almost still,
the silent dogs wound into sleep,
the gray cabins breathing steadily
in moonlight, tomorrow wakening
slowly in the clumps of mountain oak
and pine where streams once ran
down the little white rock gullies.
You can feel the whole country
wanting to waken into a child's dream,
you can feel the moment reaching
back to contain your life and forward
to whatever the dawn brings you to.
In the dark you can love this place.

The Seventh Summer

How could I not know God had a son?
the biggest kid asked. I considered.
No one told me. Did I ever go to church?
Yes, but they spoke a language I didn't
actually understand. The three stared at me.
I could have answered that it was possible
God did not have a son and that this picture
over what was to be my bed was a fake –
for one thing it wasn't a photograph,
for another it looked like an ad from *Life*,
but I was already sorry I'd said, 'Who
is he?' referring to the figure displayed
behind glass in a plain wooden frame.
What I truly wanted to know was why God
had let anyone do such a thing to his son,
nail his hands and feet to a huge wooden cross
from which he sagged in what appeared
to be less discomfort than I would have felt.
'The Jews done it,' the biggest one said, as though
reading my mind. I felt a chill run through me,
sure that once more I was going to be blamed
for what I had not done or what I'd done
but done without meaning to do, but the boys
– the oldest was sixteen, over twice my age – left
me to myself, for it was early to bed for everyone.
I lay awhile in the silent dark of the farmhouse
wandering if it could be so, that God had
a son he had let die, and if this were so why
no one had told me so that I might understand
why life could be so puzzling for all of us.
Days passed before Lars, the fourteen-year-old,
told me that it was OK, this Jesus had died
so that all of us could be saved, in the end
things turned out for the best. That was Sunday,
after the boys had returned from church –
to which I did not go –, and before we walked
into town to swim in the big public place.
I remember best how sweet was the lake water
we swam in, how I could even swallow
little gulps of it and not feel ill and how large
the bodies around me were, Lars and Sven thrashing
after the girls in their dark wool suits, the girls
squealing with mock hurt when they would catch

them up in their pale arms, for though their faces
were deeply browned their bodies were ghostly.
Sven, Lars, and Thomas, three boys as big as men,
who let me climb to their secret room beside
the hay loft, where they smoked and spoke of women,
the laughter rushing out of their great throats,
the strange words I had never heard before coughed
out in sudden spasms, and such hopes uttered
as they moved about the room in a half-dance,
half-sword-fight, calling out the magic names
of the absent girls as they stroked their own bodies
at chest and crotch or rolled on the floor
in mock death agony. August in Michigan,
the world spinning around me, my mother gone
in the grief of final loss, from which one day
she would awaken in daylight, one year
before the wars in Ethiopia, Spain, and China
could give my growing up its particular name,
and yet I sat at their table that night, head bowed
in the grace I did not say, thankful for corn,
beans, and poisonous pork, and understood it all.

On the Meeting of García Lorca and Hart Crane

Brooklyn, 1929. Of course Crane's
been drinking and has no idea who
this curious Andalusian is, unable
even to speak the language of poetry.
The young man who brought them
together knows both Spanish and English,
but he has a headache from jumping
back and forth from one language
to another. For a moment's relief
he goes to the window to look
down on the East River, darkening
below as the early night comes on.
Something flashes across his sight,
a double vision of such horror
he has to slap both his hands across
his mouth to keep from screaming.
Let's not be frivolous, let's
not pretend the two poets gave
each other wisdom or love or
even a good time, let's not
invent a dialogue of such eloquence
that even the ants in your own
house won't forget it. The two
greatest poetic geniuses alive
meet, and what happens? A vision
comes to an ordinary man staring
at a filthy river. Have you ever
had a vision? Have you ever shaken
your head to pieces and jerked back
at the image of your young son
falling through open space, not
from the stern of a ship bound
from Vera Cruz to New York but from
the roof of the building he works on?
Have you risen from bed to pace
until dawn to beg a merciless God
to take these pictures away? Oh, yes,
let's bless the imagination. It gives
us the myths we live by. Let's bless

the visionary power of the human –
the only animal that's got it –,
bless the exact image of your father
dead and mine dead, bless the images
that stalk the corners of our sight
and will not let go. The young man
was my cousin, Arthur Lieberman,
then a language student at Columbia,
who told me all this before he died
quietly in his sleep in 1983
in a hotel in Perugia. A good man,
Arthur, he survived graduate school,
later came home to Detroit and sold
pianos right through the Depression.
He loaned my brother a used one
to compose his hideous songs on,
which Arthur thought were genius.
What an imagination Arthur had!

Ask for Nothing

Instead walk alone in the evening
heading out of town toward the fields
asleep under a darkening sky;
the dust risen from your steps transforms
itself into a golden rain fallen
earthward as a gift from no known god.
The plane trees along the canal bank,
the few valley poplars, hold their breath
as you cross the wooden bridge that leads
nowhere you haven't been, for this walk
repeats itself once or more a day.
That is why in the distance you see
beyond the first ridge of low hills
where nothing ever grows, men and women
astride mules, on horseback, some even
on foot, all the lost family you
never prayed to see, praying to see you,
chanting and singing to bring the moon
down into the last of the sunlight.
Behind you the windows of the town
blink on and off, the houses close down;
ahead the voices fade like music
over deep water, and then are gone;
even the sudden, tumbling finches
have fled into smoke, and the one road
whitened in moonlight leads everywhere.

The Trade

Crouching down in the loud morning air
of the docks of Genoa, with the gulls wheeling
overhead, the fishermen calling, I considered
for a moment, then traded a copy of T.S. Eliot
for a pocket knife and two perfect lemons.
The old man who engineered the deal held
the battered black *Selected Poems*, pushed
the book out at arm's length perusing the notes
to 'The Wasteland' as though he understood them.
Perhaps he did. He sifted through the box
of lemons, sniffing the tough skins of several,
before finally settling on just that pair.
He worked the large blade back and forth
nodding all the while, and stopped abruptly
as though to say, Perfect! I had not
come all that way from America by way
of the Indies to rid myself of the burden
of a book that haunted me or even to say,
I've had it with middle age, poetry, my life.
I came only from Barcelona on the good ship
Kangaroo, sitting up on deck all night
with a company of conscript Spaniards
who passed around the black wine of Alicante
while they sang gypsy ballads and Sinatra.
We'd been six hours late getting started.
In the long May light the first beacons
along the Costa Brava came on, then France
slipped by, jewelled in the darkness, as I
dozed and drank by turns in the warm sea air
which calmed everything. A book my brother gave
twenty years before, out of love, stolen
from Doubleday's and brought to the hospital
as an offering, brother to brother, and carried
all those years until the words, memorised,
meant nothing. A grape knife, wooden handled,
fattened at one end like a dark fist, the blade
lethal and slightly rusted. Two lemons, one
for my pocket, one for my rucksack, perfuming
my clothes, my fingers, my money, my hair,
so that all the way to Rapallo on the train
I would stand among my second-class peers, tall,
angelic, an ordinary man become a gift.

Magpiety

You pull over to the shoulder
    of the two-lane
road and sit for a moment wondering
    where you were going
in such a hurry. The valley is burned
    out, the oaks
dream day and night of rain
    which never comes.
At noon or just before noon
    the short shadows
are gray and hold what little
    life survives.
In the still heat the engine
    clicks, although
the real heat is hours ahead.
    You get out and step
cautiously over a low wire
    fence and begin
the climb up the yellowed hill.
    A hundred feet
ahead the trunks of two
    fallen oaks
rust; something passes over
    them, a lizard
perhaps or a trick of sight.
    The next tree
you pass is unfamiliar,
    the trunk dark,
as black as an olive's; the low
    branches stab
out, gnarled and dull: a carob
    or a Joshua tree.
A sudden flaring-up ahead,
    a black-winged
bird rises from nowhere,
    white patches
underneath its wings, and is gone.
    You hear your own
breath catching in your ears,
    a roaring, a sea
sound that goes on and on
    until you lean
forward to place both hands
    – fingers spread –

into the bleached grasses
and let your knees
slowly down. Your breath slows
and you know
you're back in central
California
on your way to San Francisco
or the coastal towns
with their damp sea breezes
you haven't
even a hint of. But first
you must cross
the Pacheco Pass. People
expect you, and yet
you remain, still leaning forward
into the grasses
that if you could hear them
would tell you
all you need to know about
the life ahead.

Out of a sense of modesty
or to avoid the truth
I've been writing in the second
person, but in truth
it was I, not you, who pulled
the green Ford
over to the side of the road
and decided to get
up that last hill to look
back at the valley
he'd come to call home.
I can't believe
that man, only thirty-two,
less than half
my age, could be the person
fashioning these lines.
That was late July of '60.
I had heard
all about magpies, how they
snooped and meddled
in the affairs of others, not
birds so much
as people. If you dared
to remove a wedding
ring as you washed away
the stickiness of love

or the cherished odors of another
      man or woman,
as you turned away
      from the mirror
having admired your new-found
      potency – humming
'My Funny Valentine' or
      'Body and Soul' –
to reach for a rough towel
      or some garment
on which to dry yourself,
      he would enter
the open window behind you
      that gave gratefully
onto the fields and the roads
      bathed in dawn –
he, the magpie – and snatch
      up the ring
in his hard beak and shoulder
      his way back
into the currents of the world
      on his way
to the only person who could
      change your life:
a king or a bride or an old woman
      asleep on her porch.

Can you believe the bird
      stood beside you
just long enough, though far
      smaller than you
but fearless in a way
      a man or woman
could never be? An apparition
      with two dark
and urgent eyes and motions
      so quick and precise
they were barely motions at all?
      When he was gone
you turned, alarmed by the rustling
      of oily feathers
and the curious pungency,
      and were sure
you'd heard him say the words
      that could explain
the meaning of blond grasses
      burning on a hillside

beneath the hands of a man
          in the middle of
his life caught in the posture
          of prayer. I'd
heard that a magpie could talk,
          so I waited
for the words, knowing without
          the least doubt
what he'd do, for up ahead
          an old woman
waited on her wide front porch.
          My children
behind her house played
          in a silted pond
poking sticks at the slow
          carp that flashed
in the fallen sunlight. You
          are thirty-two
only once in your life, and though
          July comes
too quickly, you pray for
          the overbearing
heat to pass. It does, and
          the year turns
before it holds still for
          even a moment.
Beyond the last carob
          or Joshua tree
the magpie flashes his sudden
          wings; a second
flames and vanishes into the pale
          blue air.
July 23, 1960.
          I lean down
closer to hear the burned grasses
          whisper all I
need to know. The words rise
          around me, separate
and finite. A yellow dust
          rises and stops
caught in the noon's driving light.
          Three ants pass
across the back of my reddened
          right hand.
Everything is speaking or singing.
          We're still here.

The Poem of Chalk

On the way to lower Broadway
this morning I faced a tall man
speaking to a piece of chalk
held in his right hand. The left
was open, and it kept the beat,
for his speech had a rhythm,
was a chant or dance, perhaps
even a poem in French, for he
was from Senegal and spoke French
so slowly and precisely that I
could understand as though
hurled back fifty years to my
high school classroom. A slender man,
elegant in his manner, neatly dressed
in the remnants of two blue suits,
his tie fixed squarely, his white shirt
spotless though unironed. He knew
the whole history of chalk, not only
of this particular piece, but also
the chalk with which I wrote
my name the day they welcomed
me back to school after the death
of my father. He knew feldspar,
he knew calcium, oyster shells, he
knew what creatures had given
their spines to become the dust time
pressed into these perfect cones,
he knew the sadness of classrooms
in December when the light fails
early and the words on the blackboard
abandon their grammar and sense
and then even their shapes so that
each letter points in every direction
at once and means nothing at all.
At first I thought his short beard
was frosted with chalk; as we stood
face to face, no more than a foot
apart, I saw the hairs were white,
for though youthful in his gestures
he was, like me, an aging man, though
far nobler in appearance with his high
carved cheekbones, his broad shoulders,
and clear dark eyes. He had the bearing

of a king of lower Broadway, someone
out of the mind of Shakespeare or
García Lorca, someone for whom loss
had sweetened into charity. We stood
for that one long minute, the two
of us sharing the final poem of chalk
while the great city raged around
us, and then the poem ended, as all
poems do, and his left hand dropped
to his side abruptly and he handed
me the piece of chalk. I bowed,
knowing how large a gift this was
and wrote my thanks on the air
where it might be heard forever
below the sea shell's stiffening cry.

The Escape

To come to life in Detroit is to be manufactured
without the power of speech. You clasp hands,
as I did, with a brother and step by step
begin the slow descent into hell or Hamtramck
and arrive, designed, numbered, tagged.
It was the year Hoover took office. Since then
I've been recycled seven times and escaped
myself twice. The second time I ran my hand
down the body next to me and felt my callused hand
touching *me*. She and I hushed in a room
I rented for $12 a month down the street
from the shabby little zoo. How late I came
to love, 26 years old, and for the first time
I became a woman, a singular woman who loved me
more than I loved myself. What had I been?
What do you think? Isn't it obvious? I was a child.
And then I discovered Luckys, and then I suppose
I created out of lies, bad teeth, and so much meat,
bone, and hair a character in the shape of a man.
Then I registered for the draft and it was official.
Case closed, 1A, classified to die before I came of age
unless Hiroshima and Nagasaki burned. They did,
and I celebrated by drinking myself into a stupor
that lasted eight years.   The first time I escaped
I'd gone out after dinner and the dishes were done
to be alone. In the dark I found the tree,
a copper beech, and climbed into the crotch
and leaned back against a heavy branch and let
the stars pass slowly above. At first cars
groaned one at a time on the Outer Drive,
then they did not, and besides the wind stirring
the hard black leaves there was only the roar
of my mind touching itself carefully with rain,
the first few drops filling my eyes, that day's
rain falling hours later from the leaves above,
wind shaken, and then the odor of earth rising
like the breath of a strange God I could love.
Can you imagine inhaling God at age fourteen
with lungs still untainted by cigarettes?
Little wonder I fell out of the tree and sprawled
face down, unhurt, my fingers spread wide
as though to take handfuls of last year's

brittle leaves into my mouth. Hours later
I rose in the shape of a boy named Phil,
but now myself.
                I'm an American,
even before I was fourteen I knew I would have
to create myself. My beautiful literature teacher,
Miss Hardman, who wore gloves on summer days,
who had a secret love for me she could
barely contain, had whispered this one day
as we passed in the hall and fought to still
the urge to take my head in her ungloved hands
and press my soul into her breasts. If she
had not nursed that unacted desire
I might have discovered love before
I was ready and lost it, never to awaken
in a rented room thirteen years later
transformed into an angel gifted with both
sexes and no wings. Because we were Midwestern
someone always had to pay: Johnny Moradian
had to be blown apart on Okinawa, Silas Nance
had to despise himself before my eyes, weeping
and weeping because a woman belittled him,
Jewel Sprague had to run off to Peru and disappear
in the Andes, my tiny French cousin had to walk
by night from Nîmes to the hills freezing
above Florence to survive the Nazis and succumb
to his own heart, my lost uncle had to stab
a man to death behind a bar on First Avenue
and beg God to punish him. Oh Lord of Life,
how much you made them pay so I could love.

The Simple Truth

I bought a dollar and a half's worth of small red potatoes,
took them home, boiled them in their jackets
and ate them for dinner with a little butter and salt.
Then I walked through the dried fields
on the edge of town. In middle June the light
hung on in the dark furrows at my feet,
and in the mountain oaks overhead the birds
were gathering for the night, the jays and mockers
squawking back and forth, the finches still darting
into the dusty light. The woman who sold me
the potatoes was from Poland; she was someone
out of my childhood in a pink spangled sweater and sunglasses
praising the perfection of all her fruits and vegetables
at the roadside stand and urging me to taste
even the pale, raw sweetcorn trucked all the way,
she swore, from New Jersey. 'Eat, eat,' she said,
'Even if you don't I'll say you did.'
                                    Some things
you know all your life. They are so simple and true
they must be said without elegance, meter and rhyme,
they must be laid on the table beside the salt shaker,
the glass of water, the absence of light gathering
in the shadows of picture frames, they must be
naked and alone, they must stand for themselves.
My friend Henri and I arrived at this together in 1965
before I went away, before he began to kill himself,
and the two of us to betray our love. Can you taste
what I'm saying? It is onions or potatoes, a pinch
of simple salt, the wealth of melting butter, it is obvious,
it stays in the back of your throat like a truth
you never uttered because the time was always wrong,
it stays there for the rest of your life, unspoken,
made of that dirt we call earth, the metal we call salt,
in a form we have no words for, and you live on it.

No Buyers

Two books in Spanish
on the children of
the clouds, an electric
motor for a fan and no
fan blade, three spotted
eggs, uncracked. Bend
down and look: the eggs
are almost new. They glow
like the just born or
the just dead, feel
the heat as it passes
through your hand. Three
perfect shapes a thousand
sciences could not
improve, for sale to
anyone. A light snow
drifts down, perhaps
it's only shards of
paper, falling from
city hall, perhaps it's
light in tiny diamonds
meant to consecrate
the day or dirty it.
The keepers of this
shop – can we call them
shopkeepers, though in
the filthy air there's
nothing here to keep
except their distance
and their stillness? –
are river people. You
can tell by the way
the lines swirl away
from their eyes and race
off in all directions,
you can tell by the way
the man squats and does
not spit. Underneath,
the BMT rumbles on its
way to an ocean these two
will never see again.
The street rocks; the man
and woman hold. Garter

and panty set bunched against
the cold, the black broken
teeth of an old comb,
a plastic, satin-lined
casket for fountain pens,
a dusting of snow or more
tired paper. All these
riches set out on a blanket
from Samarkand or Toledo
that bears in black
the outline of the great
bird beneath whose wings
we flew out of the fires
of morning. A bus hisses
past for the seventh time,
sighing. A cop stops and
talks to no one, and he
sighs too. The clouds go
on clawing overhead. Children
rise from the underground
or descend in streams from
the clouds. For a moment
there is music and then not.
Light drains from above and
runs like melted lead into
the open steaming vents.
Side by side these two stand
while the day passes or
an hour passes in the almost
new dark as the three eggs
hatch into smaller and newer
eggs and nobody buys.

Edward Lieberman, Entrepreneur,
Four Years after the Burnings on Okinawa

The light sifts down from the naked bulb
he's quickened with a string. He speaks
to no one out of the well of his anger.
He says, 'I hate this,' and he stops.
He means more than this one-man shop
on Grand River where he stores the drive-
shafts, bearings, and U-joints swiped
from the Rockwell Arsenal. He means
the stalled traffic outside, the semis
barking and coughing, the gray floor
inside littered with crowded pallets
so filthy they seem furred. He means
the single desk and chair, the hat rack
holding no hats, he even means the phone
he's become so good at, for he's learned
to give nothing away that matters and still
sound serious, to say, 'No, we never
allow that much time,' and, 'Pretty good,
and you?' in a voice so deep even he
doesn't know it. Wardie, everyone's cousin,
still in his twenties, though the blue-
black double-breasted size forty-six he strains
against makes him look forty, the hard fat
of neck, upper chest, and shoulders draws
him down into the chair, and he swivels
abruptly toward those he can't see. Go ahead,
reach out and stroke the dark stubble,
run a lone cautious finger down the channels
for the tears he spills only in sleep.
He won't bite you. He's Wardie, the lost
brother no one remembers, so give him
the love he can't give himself. Feel him
shudder and draw back, not because he kept
his word and killed, not because your thought
became his act, but because it came to this.

My Father with Cigarette Twelve Years
Before the Nazis Could Break His Heart

I remember the room in which he held
a kitchen match and with his thumbnail
commanded it to flame: a brown sofa,
two easy chairs, one covered with flowers,
a black piano no one ever played half
covered by a long-fringed ornamental scarf
Ray Estrada brought back from Mexico
in 1931. How new the world is, you say.
In that room someone is speaking about money,
asking why it matters, and my father exhales
the blue smoke, and says a million dollars
even in large bills would be impossible.
He's telling me because, I see now, I'm
the one who asked, for I dream of money,
always coins and bills that run through my hands,
money I find in the corners of unknown rooms
or in metal boxes I dig up in the backyard
flower beds of houses I've never seen.
My father rises now and goes to the closet.
It's as though someone were directing a play
and my father's part called for him to stand
so that the audience, which must be you,
could see him in white shirt, dark trousers,
held up by suspenders, a sign of the times,
and conclude he is taller than his son
will ever be, and as he dips into his jacket,
you'll know his role calls for him to exit
by the front door, leaving something
unfinished, the closet light still on,
the cigarette still burning dangerously,
a Yiddish paper folded to the right place
so that a photograph of Hindenburg
in full military regalia swims up
to you out of all the details we lived.
I remember the way the match flared
blue and yellow in the deepening light
of a cool afternoon in early September,
and the sound, part iron, part animal,
part music, as the air rushed toward it
out of my mouth, and his intake of breath
through the Lucky Strike, and the smoke
hanging on after the door closed and the play

ran out of acts and actors, and the audience –
which must be you – grew tired of these lives
that finally come to nothing or no more
than the furniture and the cotton drapes
left open so the darkening sky can seem
to have the last word, with half a moon
and a showering of fake stars to say what
the stars always say about the ordinary.
Oh, you're still here, 60 years later,
you wonder what became of us, why
someone put it in a book, and left
the book open to a page no one reads.
Everything tells you he never came back,
though he did before he didn't, everything
suggests it was the year Hitler came
to power, the year my grandmother learned
to read English novels and fell in love
with *David Copperfield* and *Oliver Twist*
which she read to me seated on a stool
beside my bed until I fell asleep.
Everything tells you this is a preface
to something important, the Second World War,
the news that leaked back from Poland
that the villages were gone. The truth is –
if there is a truth – I remember the room,
I remember the flame, the blue smoke,
how bright and slippery were the secret coins,
how David Copperfield doubted his own name,
how sweet the stars seemed, peeping and blinking
how close the moon, how utterly silent the piano.

Smoke

Can you imagine the air filled with smoke?
It was. The city was vanishing before noon
or was it earlier than that? I can't say because
the light came from nowhere and went nowhere.

This was years ago, before you were born, before
your parents met in a bus station downtown.
She'd come on Friday after work all the way
from Toledo, and he'd dressed in his only suit.

Back then we called this a date, sometimes
a blind date, though they'd written back and forth
for weeks. What actually took place is now lost.
It's become part of the mythology of a family,

the stories told by children around the dinner table.
No, they aren't dead, they're just treated that way,
as objects turned one way and then another
to catch the light, the light overflowing with smoke.

Go back to the beginning, you insist. Why
is the air filled with smoke? Simple. We had work.
Work was something that thrived on fire, that without
fire couldn't catch its breath or hang on for life.

We came out into the morning air, Bernie, Stash,
Williams, and I, it was late March, a new war
was starting up in Asia or closer to home,
one that meant to kill us, but for a moment

the air held still in the gray poplars and elms
undoing their branches. I understood the moon
for the very first time, why it came and went, why
it wasn't there that day to greet the four of us.

Before the bus came a small black bird settled
on the curb, fearless or hurt, and turned its beak up
as though questioning the day. 'A baby crow,'
someone said. Your father knelt down on the wet cement,

his lunchbox balanced on one knee and stared quietly
for a long time. 'A grackle far from home,' he said.
One of the four of us mentioned *tenderness*,
a word I wasn't used to, so it wasn't me.

The bus must have arrived. I'm not there today.
The windows were soiled. We swayed this way and that
over the railroad tracks, across Woodward Avenue,
heading west, just like the sun, hidden in smoke.

Reinventing America

The city was huge. A boy of twelve could walk
for hours while the closed houses stared down at him
from early morning to dusk, and he'd get nowhere.
Oh no, I was not that boy. Even at twelve I knew
enough to stay in my own neighborhood,
I knew anyone who left might not return.
Boys were animals with animal hungers
I learned early. Better to stay close to home.
I'd try to bum cigarettes from the night workers
as they left the bars in the heavy light of noon
or I'd hang around the grocery hoping
one of the beautiful young wives would ask me
to help her carry her shopping bags home.
You're wondering what I was up to. Not much.
The sun rose late in November and set early.
At times I thought life was rushing by too fast.
Before I knew it I'd be my half-blind uncle
married to a woman who cried all day long
while in the basement he passed his time working
on short-wave radio calls to anywhere.
I'd sneak down and talk to him. Uncle Nathan,
wiry in his boxer's shorts and high-topped boots,
chewing on a cigar, the one dead eye catching
the overhead light while he mused on his life
on the road or at sea. How he loved the whores
in the little Western towns or the Latin ports!
He'd hold his hands out to approximate
their perfect breasts. The months in jail had taught him
a man had only his honor and his ass
to protect. 'You turn your fist this way,' he said,
taking my small hand in both of his, 'and fire
from the shoulder, so,' and he'd extend it out
to the face of an imaginary foe.
Why he'd returned to this I never figured out,
though life was ample here, a grid of crowded blocks
of Germans, Wops, Polacks, Jews, wild Irish,
plus some square heads from the Upper Peninsula.
Six bakeries, four barber shops, a five and dime
twenty beer gardens, a Catholic church with a *shul*
next door where we studied the Talmud-Torah.
Wonderful how all the old hatreds bubbled
so quietly on the back burner you could
forget until one day they tore through the pool halls,

the bowling alley, the high school athletic fields
leaving an eye gone, a long fresh, livid scar
running to touch a mouth, young hands raw or broken,
boys and girls ashamed of what they were, ashamed
of what they were not. It was merely village life,
exactly what our parents left in Euope
brought to America with pure fidelity.

Salt and Oil

Three young men in dirty work clothes
on their way home or to a bar
in the late morning. This is not
a photograph, it is a moment
in the daily life of the world,
a moment that will pass into
the unwritten biography
of your city or my city
unless it is frozen in the fine print
of our eyes. I turn away
to read the morning paper and lose
the words. I go into the streets
for an hour or more, walking slowly
for even a man of my age. I buy
an apple but do not eat it.
The old woman who sells it remarks
on its texture and tartness, she
laughs and the veins of her cheeks brown.
I stare into the river while time
refuses to move. Meanwhile the three
begin to fade, giving up
their names and voices, their auras
of smoke and grease, their acrid bouquets.
We shall name one to preserve him,
we shall name him *Salt*, the tall blond
whose wrists hurt, who is holding back
something, curses or tears, and shaking
out the exhaustion, his blue eyes
swollen with sleeplessness, his words
blasted on the horn of his breath.
We could go into the cathedral
of his boyhood and recapture
the voices that were his, we could
reclaim him from the brink of fire,
but then we would lose the other,
the one we call *Oil*, for Oil
broods in the tiny crevices
between then and now. Oil survives
in the locked archives of the clock.
His one letter proclaims, 'My Dear
President, I would rather not...'
One arm draped across the back
of Salt, his mouth wide with laughter,

the black hair blurring the forehead,
he extends his right hand, open
and filthy to take rusted chains,
frozen bearings, the scarred hands
of strangers, there is nothing
he will not take. These two are not
brothers, the one tall and solemn,
the long Slavic nose, the pale eyes,
the puffed mouth offended by the press
of traffic, while the twin is glad
to be with us on this late morning
in paradise. If you asked him,
'Do you calm the roiling waters?'
he would smile and shake his great head,
unsure of your meaning. If you asked
the sources of his glee he would shrug
his thick shoulders and roll his eyes
upward to where the turning leaves
take the wind, and the gray city birds
dart toward their prey, and flat clouds
pencil their obscure testaments
on the air. For a moment
the energy that makes them who
they are shatters the noon's light
into our eyes, and when we see
again they are gone and the street
is quiet, the day passing into
evening, and this is autumn
in the present year. 'The third man,'
you ask, 'who was the third man
in the photograph?' There is no
photograph, no mystery,
only Salt and Oil
in the daily round of the world,
three young men in dirty work clothes
on their way under a halo
of torn clouds and famished city birds.
There is smoke and grease, there is
the wrist's exhaustion, there is laughter,
there is the letter seized in the clock
and the apple's tang, the river
sliding along its banks, darker
now than the sky descending
a last time to scatter its diamonds
into these black waters that contain
the day that passed, the night to come.

Sundays with Lungo

Lungo and I would go into the deep woods
on Sunday mornings before the town woke.
I think he was looking for something rare,
a sign maybe, a stream carved from gray snow,
wild wisteria that grows like weeds down here,
or perhaps a pale crocus or robin eggs.
You couldn't tell with Lungo, he said so little,
and what he said came sideways out of his mouth
so the wind would blow it to tatters, words
that became nothing. He'd stop abruptly,
drop to one knee, move a few twigs and leaves,
then rise and go on. It was his mission,
I liked to think, and I was simply there
as the witness to his perseverance.
We'd go on until we broke into light
at the river's edge. On the other side
more dark woods stood as a silent rebuke
to Lungo's quest, if quest it was. He'd shake
his great white head, and the laughter would burst
like song from his thin chest, for we were stopped.
No, we weren't boys. We were men, not young men
either though young men do useless things
year after year for the sake of doing.
Before he died I knew what was coming
because in those last weeks I heard his voice
suddenly surging and roaring, not words,
or at least not words I knew, just pure sounds
thrust back into the wind's face, and his face –
already deeply carved – darkened with joy.
That last Sunday when we found the river
rain was falling softly into the leaves
behind us, and the gray waters swept by
hiding their mysteries and the far woods
glistened with promise. 'This is it,' he said,
and dropped to both knees and closed his eyes up
so tightly not a single tear escaped.
I came back once, alone, looking for him,
for all he spoke or beckoned to, and found
something familiar. I stopped long before
I reached the river; the wind was speaking
in the top branches of the sycamores
telling me he was here if anywhere.
Do you know how to read the wind? Do you?

It's easy. Just close your eyes and listen.
Of course you have to be old, broken
in body and spirit, brought down so low –
as Lungo was – that even words make sense.

Philosophy Lesson

After driving all night long
I stopped for coffee and eggs
at a diner halfway to
New York City. The waitress
behind the counter looked up
from her magazine and said,
'Look who's here!' clapped her hands
together and broke into
a huge smile. 'Have I been here
before?' I asked. 'Beats the shit
out of me,' she said and put
a glass of cloudy water
in front of me. 'What'll it be?'
One war was closing down
in Asia to be followed
by another. No longer
a kid, I wondered who was
I that a gray-haired woman
up all night in a road-side
hole would greet me like a star.
'What do you think of Sartre
and the Existentialists?'
I asked. 'We get the eggs fresh
from down the road, my old man
bakes the bread and sweet rolls.
It's all good.' It's not often
you get the perfect answer
to such a profound question.
On the way back to the truck
I listened to the pebbles
crunching under my wing-tips,
watched two huge crows watching me
from a sad maple, smelled
the fishy air blowing in
from Lake Erie, and thought, 'Some
things are too good to be true.'

Cesare

One sorry town after another passed
the streaked windows of the train. We smoked, talk
of growing up, he near Torino,
I in Michigan. Born in a small town
in an inland valley, he loved the sea,
just walking along the shore, day or night,
filled with a joy he'd never known.
In my imagination even in the rain,
with his wool cap pulled down over one eye,
he passes the window of the café
like a ghost as the day fails. I see him
coming toward me now, tall, thin, myopic,
full of delight in his awkward body,
still only a boy with a boy's wide smile
as the rain streams down. You too must know
men like Cesare, still so young, brilliant,
full of plans and tall tales. Then women
enter their lives and the unfillable need
for tenderness. They fall in love, then
fall in love again and again and nothing
comes of it but heartbreak. And they are men,
so when you reach to touch them, to help them,
they turn away because men must do that.
Of course I never knew any Cesare,
he died before I left Detroit, before
I had a chance. I'm really talking
about someone else I can't name because
I simply can't, a man so singular
that when I lost him I had the train ride
I couldn't forget, Paris to somewhere
in early fall, the towns along the way
with their blackened churches, factories, shops,
cinemas all closed down. How did I miss
what was to come? It was all there in the rain.

The Return

All afternoon my father drove the country roads
between Detroit and Lansing. What he was looking for
I never learned, no doubt because he never knew himself,
though he would grab any unfamiliar side road
and follow where it led past fields of tall sweet corn
in August or in winter those of frozen sheaves.
Often he'd leave the Terraplane beside the highway
to enter the stunned silence of mid-September,
his eyes cast down for a sign, the only music
his own breath or the wind tracking slowly through
the stalks or riding above the barren ground. Later
he'd come home, his dress shoes coated with dust or mud,
his long black overcoat stained or tattered
at the hem, sit wordless in his favorite chair,
his necktie loosened, and stare at nothing. At first
my brothers and I tried conversation, questions
only he could answer: Why had he gone to war?
Where did he learn Arabic? Where was his father?
I remember none of this. I read it all later,
years later as an old man, a grandfather myself,
in a journal he left my mother with little drawings
of ruined barns and telephone poles, receding
toward a future he never lived, aphorisms
from Montaigne, Juvenal, Voltaire, and perhaps a few
of his own: 'He who looks for answers finds questions.'
Three times he wrote, 'I was meant to be someone else,'
and went on to describe the perfumes of the damp fields.
'It all starts with seeds,' and a pencil drawing
of young apple trees he saw somewhere or else dreamed.

I inherited the book when I was almost seventy
and with it the need to return to who we were.
In the Detroit airport I rented a Taurus;
the woman at the counter was bored or crazy:
Did I want company? she asked; she knew every road
from here to Chicago. She had a slight accent,
Dutch or German, long black hair, and one frozen eye.
I considered but decided to go alone,
determined to find what he had never found.
Slowly the autumn morning warmed, flocks of starlings
rose above the vacant fields and blotted out the sun.
I drove on until I found the grove of apple trees
heavy with fruit, and left the car, the motor running,

beside a sagging fence, and entered his life
on my own for maybe the first time. A crow welcomed
me home, the sun rode above, austere and silent,
the early afternoon was cloudless, perfect.
When the crow dragged itself off to another world,
the shade deepened slowly in pools that darkened around
the trees; for a moment everything in sight stopped.
The wind hummed in my good ear, not words exactly,
not nonsense either, nor what I spoke to myself,
just the language creation once wakened to.
I took off my hat, a mistake in the presence
of my father's God, wiped my brow with what I had,
the back of my hand, and marveled at what was here:
nothing at all except the stubbornness of things.

The Mercy

The ship that took my mother to Ellis Island
Eighty-three years ago was named 'The Mercy'.
She remembers trying to eat a banana
without first peeling it and seeing her first orange
in the hands of a young Scot, a seaman
who gave her a bite and wiped her mouth for her
with a red bandana and taught her the word,
'orange', saying it patiently over and over.
A long autumn voyage, the days darkening
with the black waters calming as night came on,
then nothing as far as her eyes could see and space
without limit rushing off to the corners
of creation. She prayed in Russian and Yiddish
to find her family in New York, prayers
unheard or misunderstood or perhaps ignored
by all the powers that swept the waves of darkness
before she woke, that kept 'The Mercy' afloat
while smallpox raged among the passengers
and crew until the dead were buried at sea
with strange prayers in a tongue she could not fathom.
'The Mercy', I read on the yellowing pages of a book
I located in a windowless room of the library
on 42nd Street, sat thirty-one days
offshore in quarantine before the passengers
disembarked. There a story ends. Other ships
arrived, 'Tancred' out of Glasgow, 'The Neptune'
registered as Danish, 'Umberto IV',
the list goes on for pages, November gives
way to winter, the sea pounds this alien shore.
Italian miners from Piemonte dig
under towns in western Pennsylvania
only to rediscover the same nightmare
they left at home. A nine-year-old girl travels
all night by train with one suitcase and an orange.
She learns that mercy is something you can eat
again and again while the juice spills over
your chin, you can wipe it away with the back
of your hands and you can never get enough.

Gospel

The new grass rising in the hills,
the cows loitering in the morning chill,
a dozen or more old browns hidden
in the shadows of the cottonwoods
beside the streambed. I go higher
to where the road gives up and there's
only a faint path strewn with lupine
between the mountain oaks. I don't
ask myself what I'm looking for.
I didn't come for answers
to a place like this, I came to walk
on the earth, still cold, still silent.
Still ungiving, I've said to myself,
although it greets me with last year's
dead thistles and this year's
hard spines, early-blooming
wild onions, the curling remains
of spider's cloth. What did I bring
to the dance? In my back pocket
a crushed letter from a woman
I've never met bearing bad news
I can do nothing about. So I wander
these woods half sightless while
a west wind picks up in the trees
clustered above. The pines make
a music like no other, rising and
falling like a distant surf at night
that calms the darkness before
first light. 'Soughing' we call it, from
Old English, no less. How weightless
words are when nothing will do.

The Great Truth

Early Sunday morning he'd drive the black Packard
to the 'island' – as he called it – a public park
in the Detroit River, and walk slowly
along the horse paths, both hands clasped
together behind his back. He always wore the good gray suit,
white shirt stiffly starched, black polished wing-tips.
Why the horse paths, I wondered, that led us away
from the river, the broad view of the skyline,
the ore boats headed toward unknown, exotic ports,
why into the silent darkened woods, fringed
with nettled scrub and echoing with crow calls.
The September he came back from prison, penniless,
and took a murderous night job in the forge room
at Cadillac, he'd rise before dawn to waken me
in the still house. Whatever he was looking for
he never said, and I was too young to ask.
Eleven then, a growing boy, I believed
there were answers. I believed one morning
he'd turn suddenly to tell me why men and boys
went into such forbidding places or pacing
beside him, I would see some transformation
up ahead where the sky, faceless and gray, hung
above the pin oaks, and know for once the world
was not the world, that the breath battering
my ears and catching in my chest was more
than only my breath. I'd know all this was
something else, something unnamable
that included me.
                    That first Sunday no one entered
my room in the December dark to touch me
on the shoulder, I slept till almost noon.
The Packard gone, I thought, and Uncle Nate –
as I'd taken to calling him – gone as well.
I found him in shirtsleeves shoveling last night's snow
off the front steps and singing hillbilly songs.
The house is still there, one of those ghost houses
from another era with mock turrets and steep eaves
the tourists photograph. It sits on a block
of rubble and nothing waiting for JFK
to come back from Dallas and declare a new
New Frontier. The last time I saw Uncle Nate
was seventeen years ago in a bar on Linwood
with a woman anxious to leave. I had to

tell him who I was, 'Phil from the old house
on Riopelle.' He put his head down on the bar,
closed his eyes, and said, 'Oh my God, oh my God,'
and nothing more. Yesterday morning my brother
drove me out to the island. It was raining
and he waited with coffee and the *Free Press*
in the echoing rotunda while I walked
the old trails, rutted now by tire tracks, the ground
spongy and alive in April. I felt foolish
under a huge black umbrella, but no one else
was out to see me, so I went on into a stand
of new spruce and hemlock gleaming in the rain
that drummed softly into last year's dead needles.
Up ahead what little I could see of sky
lightened as though urging me toward something
waiting for me more than half a century, some
great truth to live by now that it was too late
to live in the world other than I do.

On 52nd Street

Down sat Bud, raised his hands,
the Deuces silenced, the lights
lowered, and breath gathered
for the coming storm. Then nothing,
not a single note. Outside starlight
from heaven fell unseen, a quarter-
moon, promised, was no show,
ditto the rain. Late August of '50,
NYC, the long summer of abundance
and our new war. In the mirror behind
the bar, the spirits – imitating us –
stared at themselves. At the bar
the tenor player up from Philly shut
his eyes and whispered to no one,
'Same thing last night.' Everyone
been coming all week long
to hear *this*. The big brown bass
sighed and slumped against
the piano, the cymbals held
their dry cheeks and stopped
chicking and chucking. We went
back to drinking and ignored
the unignorable. When the door
swung open, it was Pettiford
in work clothes, midnight suit,
starched shirt, narrow black tie,
spit-shined shoes, as ready
as he'd ever be. Eyebrows
raised, the Irish bartender
shook his head, so Pettiford eased
himself down at an empty table,
closed up his *Herald Tribune*,
and shook his head. Did the TV
come on, did the jukebox bring us
Dinah Washington, did the stars
keep their appointments, did the moon
show, quartered or full, sprinkling
its soft light down? The night's
still there, just where it was, just
where it'll always be without
its music. You're still there too,
holding your breath. Bud walked out.

Keats in California

The wisteria has come and gone, the plum trees
have burned like candles in the cup of earth,
the almond has shed its pure blossoms
in a soft ring around the trunk. Iris,
rose, tulip, hillsides of poppy and lupine,
gorse, wild mustard, California is blazing
in the foolish winds of April. I have been
reading Keats – the poems, the letters, the life –
for the first time in my 70th year, and I
have been watching television after dinner
as though it could bring me some obscure,
distant sign of hope. This morning I rose
late to the soft light off the eucalyptus
and the overbearing odor of orange blossoms.
The trees will give another year. They are giving.
The few, petty clouds will blow away
before noon, and we will have sunshine
without fault, china blue skies, and the bees
gathering to splatter their little honey dots
on my windshield. If I drive to the foothills
I can see fields of wildflowers on fire until
I have to look away from so much life.
I could ask myself, Have I made a Soul
today, have I sucked at the teat of the Heart
flooded with the experience of a world like ours?
Have I become a man one more time? At twenty
it made sense. I put down *The Collected Poems*,
left the reserve room of the Wayne library
to wander the streets of Detroit under a gray
soiled sky. It was spring there too, and the bells
rang at noon. The outpatients from Harper
waited timidly under the great stone cross
of the Presbyterian church for the trolley
on Woodward Avenue, their pinched faces flushed
with terror. The black tower tilted in the wind
as though it too were coming down. It made sense.
Before dark I'll feel the lassitude enter
first my arms and legs and spread like water
toward the deep organs. I'll lie on my bed
hearing the quail bark as they scurry from
cover to cover in their restless searching
after sustenance. This place can break your heart.

The Two

When he gets off work at Packard, they meet
outside a diner on Grand Boulevard. He's tired,
a bit depressed, and smelling the exhaustion
on his own breath, he kisses her carefully
on her left cheek. Early April, and the weather
has not decided if this is spring, winter, or what.
The two gaze upward at the sky, which gives
nothing away: the low clouds break here and there
and let in tiny slices of a pure blue heaven.
The day is like us, she thinks; it hasn't decided
what to become. The traffic light at Linwood
goes from red to green and the trucks start up,
so that when he says, 'Would you like to eat?'
she hears a jumble of words that means nothing,
though spiced with things she cannot believe,
'wooden Jew' and 'lucky meat'. He's been up
late, she thinks, he's tired of the job, perhaps tired
of their morning meetings, but then he bows
from the waist and holds the door open
for her to enter the diner, and the thick
odor of bacon frying and new potatoes
greets them both, and taking heart she enters
to peer through the thick cloud of tobacco smoke
to see if 'their booth' is available.
F. Scott Fitzgerald wrote that there were no
second acts in America, but he knew neither
this man nor this woman and no one else
like them unless he stayed late at the office
to test his famous one-liner, 'We keep you clean
in Muscatine', on the woman emptying
his wastebasket. Fitzgerald never wrote
with someone present, except for this woman
in a gray uniform whose comings and goings
went unnoticed even on those December evenings
she worked late while the snow fell silently
on the windowsills and the new fluorescent lights
blinked on and off. Get back to the two, you say.
Not who ordered poached eggs, who ordered
only toast and coffee, who shared the bacon
with the other, but what became of the two
when this poem ended, whose arms held whom,
who first said 'I love you' and truly meant it,
and who misunderstood the words, so longed

for and yet still so unexpected, and began
suddenly to scream and curse until the waitress
asked them both to leave. The Packard plant closed
years before I left Detroit, the diner was burned
to the ground in '67, two years before my oldest son
fled to Sweden to escape the American dream.
'And the lovers?' you ask. I wrote nothing about lovers.
Take a look. Clouds, trucks, traffic lights, a diner, work,
a wooden shoe, East Moline, poached eggs, the perfume
of frying bacon, the chaos of language, the spices
of spent breath after eight hours of night work.
Can you hear all I feared and never dared to write?
Why the two are more real than either you or me,
why I never returned to keep them in my life,
how little I now mean to myself or anyone else,
what any of this could mean, where you found
the patience to endure these truths and confusions?

My Brother, Antonio, the Baker

Did the wind blow that night? When did it not?
I'd ask you if you hadn't gone underground
lugging the answer with you.
Twenty-eight years old, on our way home
after a twelve-hour shift baking Wonder bread
for the sleeping prisoners in the drunk tank
at the Canfield Station dreaming of a breakfast
of horse cock and mattress stuffing.
(Oh, the luxuries of 1955! How fully we lived –
the working classes and the law-abiding dregs –
on buttered toast and grilled-cheese sandwiches
as the nation braced itself for pâté and pasta.)
To myself I smelled like a new mother minus
the aura of talcum and the airborne acrid aromas
of cotton diapers. Today I'd be labeled
nurturing and bountiful instead
of vegetal and weird. A blurred moon was out,
we both saw it; I know because, leaning back,
eyes closed on a ruined sky, you did your thing
welcoming the 'bright orb' waning in the west,
'Moon that rained down its silver coins
on the darkened Duero and the sleeping fields
of Soria.' Did I look like you, my face
anonymous and pure, bleached with flour,
my eyes glistening with the power of neon light
or self-love? Two grown men, side by side,
one babbling joyfully to the universe
that couldn't care less, while the other
practiced for middle age. A single crow settled
on the boiler above the Chinese restaurant,
his feathers riffling, and I took it for a sign.
A second sign was the couple exiting
the all-night pharmacy; the man came first
through the glass door, a small white sack in hand,
and let the door swing shut. Then she appeared,
one hand covering her eyes to keep
the moonlight at bay. They stood not talking
while he looked first left, then right, then left
again as flakes of darkness sifted upward
toward the streetlight. The place began to rumble
as though this were the end. You spoke again,
only this time you described someone humble
walking alone in darkness. I could see

162

the streetcar turning off Joy Road,
swaying down the tracks toward us,
its windows on fire. There must have been a wind,
a west wind. What else could have blown
the aura of forsythia through the town
and materialised one crosstown streetcar
never before on time? A spring wind
freighted with hope. I remember
thinking that at last you might shut up.
An old woman stood to give you
her seat as though you were angelic
or pregnant. When her eyes spilled over
with happiness, I saw she took your words
to heart as I never could. Maybe she recalled
the Duero, the fields asleep in moonlight,
maybe the words were music to her,
original and whole, words that took her home
to Soria or Kraków or wherever,
maybe she was not an old woman at all
but an oracle in drag who saw you as you were
and saw, too, you couldn't last the night.

Our Reds

Let us bless the three wild Reds
of our school days. Bless how easily
gaunt Vallejo would lose control,
the blood rushing to his depleted face
while his mistress in a torn trench coat
stroked his padded shoulders to calm him.
We'll call him Vallejo after the poet
only because he vaulted into speech
in such a headlong rush. (In truth
his name was Slovakian.) We'll call
her Lupino after the film star
because she was more beautiful
in memory than in fact, her cheeks
drawn over fine bones, her hair
tumbling down from under the beret,
hair we loved and called 'dirty blond'.
Vallejo would rise in class, unasked,
to interrupt 'the tired fascist swill'
the stunned professor was giving out:
'The proper function of a teacher
is to inform the unformed cadres
of the exploited classes regarding
the nature of their enslavement
to an estate sold to the masters
of the means of production.' Lupino
would rise quietly beside him to show
solidarity and to begin
her therapy. Two-ton Cohen would
join in flashing his party cards
for all to see and invoking
the sacred triads of Hegel. And we,
the unformed and uninformed, dropped
our pencils and groaned with gladness
to be quit of Aristotle's *Ethics*,
or the monetary theories
of James K. Polk, and stared into
a future of rotund potential
fulfilled. They are gone now, the three
– Vallejo, Lupino, Cohen –
into an America no one wanted
or something even worse, so bless
their certainties, their fiery voices
we so easily resisted, their tired eyes,

their cheeks flushed with sudden blood,
bless their rhetoric, bless their zeal,
bless their costumes and their cards,
bless their faith in us, especially
that faith, that hideous innocence.

Houses in Order

In cardboard boxes under the Williamsburg Bridge
a congregation of mature rats founds a new order
based on the oldest religious principle: they eat
whatever they can get their teeth into. By day
they move slowly about their kingdom, some days
so slowly they seem for hours on end to become
holy relics or the stained brown backgrounds
to events foretold in parables to do with
the savor of salt, the mysteries of mustard seeds,
meat, bones, loaves, and fishes. When you look
back they've gone into water or air, they've joined
the falling rain that makes vision so difficult
even for the visionary. The little houses keep
their secrets the way windowless houses always do,
though their walls and roofs proclaim the hour's
holy names – Nike and Converse, Panasonic and Walk-
man – and though they let light leak in through
their teeth-torn ports and darkness out from under
their lids, they're closed to all but the eyes
of the faithful. These dull pilgrims contemplate
the business of gathering and hunting while the day
hangs on and the traffic drones on the bridge above.
Soon the headlights come on, singly or in pairs,
the rain gleams through the taut cables,
no moon rises above the island where now they are
among us, each one doing a morsel of God's work
until their small jaws ache from so much prayer.

Dust

I

My wife tells me that when she was six
she came home from school to an empty house,
put down her lunch box, sat on a hassock
by her father's chair, and simply waited.
Someone known would return home soon, she was sure.
The house was still, silent, holding its breath,
the late-afternoon sunlight streamed in
the unshaded windows and turned the dust
into tiny golden planets floating
before her. Sixty-four years later
she declares, 'It was beautiful,' and goes
on to describe the sense of awe and peace
before this vision of the universe
that descended from nowhere or perhaps
rose from within. North-central Iowa,
1933, her grandmother's house.
Nothing else remains of the day. She gazes
into space seeing again those whirling
worlds more perfectly than the room she's in,
her smile open, her glazed eyes radiant.

II

A woman who thought she loved me once wrote
a story in which 'dust motes danced on and on'.
It may have had a narrative, I forget.
It may have even had some characters,
men and women or domestic animals
going about their made-up lives. I remember
the story won a prize, was published, brought
her momentary attention and money
enough to take me to lunch. I hated
the way she ate, her clothed arms close to her sides,
one hand clutching a napkin with which
she feverishly dabbed at her lips as though
ingesting her chicken salad were an act
against God or some vast cosmic principle.
When I looked at my own right hand that held
a soggy golden french fry, I saw the nails
begrimed with grease, the yellow calluses
thick on my palm and cracked fingers, and felt
spectacularly pleased simply to be me,
a dirty Detroit Jew with bad manners.

167

III

'Without our bodies we cannot love,'
someone once wrote. On my 70th birthday
my wife asks me what I want. I do not
have long to consider. 'Just you,' I say.
I live now across from a funeral parlor
where even on Sunday mornings the hearses
are taken out and first hosed down for hours,
then dried carefully and polished, slick black
'88 Lincolns tailored for their jobs
so that the dead of North Carolina
can be smoothly and dustlessly chartered
to their carved earthen holes. The gnarled old man
who commands hose and chamois wears yellow boots
his black jeans tucked inside, spits tobacco juice
while singing hoarsely. 'Can you smell the pulp mill?'
he once asked when I went out to fetch the paper.
'When the wind's wrong, they tell me it's bad.'
Scarlet fever had killed his sense of smell
in childhood, and he now counts himself lucky
in his line of work on these warm winter days.

IV

One late-winter afternoon, waiting alone
to see a friend, I wrote 'Dust Me' with my finger
on the huge green leaf of an elephant ear
in her cozy sunroom. The little request
would remain as long as the plant remained, somehow
etched in my script. Years passed before my friend
told me how deeply her mother had been hurt
by this thoughtless act I in my merriment
thought clever. I remember Mrs Kurian
later answering the door without a smile,
her eyes cast down, no doubt doing her best
to forgive me. She died and was mourned
by her five daughters. I remember my friend
sat by the deathbed thinking, My mother
is not here. Alone, the father hung on,
determined, though the house was looted, and he
mugged in his own driveway. A proud man, Roy,
he died in a rest home in San Jose
among strangers years after the house was sold
to a city councilman who raised pigs
illegally in spotless pens in the backyard.

V

On a TV spectacular the cosmos
spins like a snow shower in a light show
of heavenly bodies. I'm reminded of Dust Bowl
photographs in *Life* magazine: a farmer
and his woman run toward shelter while the earth
they tore some living from rises against them
with all its plenitude. The man and woman
are not driven from their garden in shame
as in a painting, their mouths broken with moans.
These two borrow a Ford with bad tires and worse spares;
they have themselves and three kids to feed, and so
like the wind they head west where perhaps the land
has settled down, decided to be merely
the land they'll someday take up living in.
Even the atom may be largely empty space,
the TV says. Einstein and Niels Bohr quarrel
for days and resolve nothing. Tonight my wife
holds a glass of black Catalan wine up
to the candlelight and drinks to my New Year
and I to hers, acts as good as any
to stall our time from whirling into dust.

1/1/2000

In Joe Pryskulnik's darkened kitchen the face
of Jesus appears on a dish towel, but no one's awake
to bear witness. Next door to the fenced truck yard
behind my father's grease shop where all time stopped
there's a hive of activity. You're thinking
the rats found a wolverine or the guard dogs
caught another kid strung out on crack. You're thinking
two thousand years passed in the blink of an eye
and changed nothing, the eaters went on eating,
their crazed teeth clicking with delight. You're thinking
that's my mother rising from the ashes of her years,
her robes signed with axle grease, her hair stained
by the new dawn. It's not. It's not J.P. either,
for Joe's gone west in a box, it's not my father
come back after sixty-seven years in the wrong direction,
into the earth that gagged on motor oil, the earth
that gave back wild phlox, flags, weeds, unasked
for each April. You're thinking the dawn won't break,
that time will end because it must, and the face of Christ
will blaze in the darkness of a loveless century
while the cat and the mouse slumber side by side
in this impossible kingdom. Tomorrow is on
the way, an hour ago the sun broke through
the thatched roof of Rassan the Messenger,
scarring the silent forehead on which the ants
replayed their games. Before you can blink, the light
will blister the gray hair of Margaret Baxter
to reveal two hands swollen like potatoes and crossed
on her breast. Let Scotland mourn her loss,
let the waves off Scapa Flow work less and less
as the departed join the patient families
of the drowned. Let us honor her life with a feast
of potatoes, the million and one she scrubbed
and peeled, and garlic and onion for Andrés,
those fruits of his labor, of his one lifetime
in Haskell, New Jersey, where now he resides
in Rousek's Catholic Funeral Home without *paz*,
dolor, *merced*, with no one to speak his name
or sing him lullabies. Let the new day
break on the fenced yard, let it fill the kitchen
with light overflowing the stained shot glass
Joe left behind, the grail of his hopes, let it rust
with animal blood the blurred face of Jesus

on the Shroud of Michigan and westward move
across blackened Gary, the frozen prairies,
the great divide, to find us in the valleys
of our living where we surrendered our names
and natures, with all that made us human, let it
go on, this empty fraction of eternity,
to die at last in the ocean of its birth.

My Father in the Wind

Even in the dark the wind blows. I hear it
in the high branches of the great cedar
humming its one tune. In the small room
that is mine the dust grains refuse to speak
although they know it all, for they contain
the ashes of my father, being far older
than time, and the singular pain of his father
who took his own life and left his son
no final word, only silence and an open door
through which the boy – my father – discovered
the unfamiliar humped shadow swinging
in no wind. Orphaned, the boy did not
sit down by the waters of the Dnieper to weep
as a man might do in a sacred text, he did not
curse God or howl or simply stand stunned
by the bright sun's arrival on such a day
or even beg a neighbor to cut down
the body. He climbed a ladder, braced his legs
against the top rung, and with a rusted saw
and one hand guiding the blade,
the other pulling through the golden bands
of sisal, slowly severed whatever
connected his father's body to its final act.

You might well ask how I know all this
since the dust that was there is silent still.
You think my father never spoke? You think
because he was tall, dark–suited, responsible,
and I was a kid he wouldn't turn suddenly
when the traffic stalled and address me
as he might address the wind? He would be dust.
He'd learned that twenty years before on that day
in Dobrovica in autumn, the day the wind called
to him from the plane trees flanking the river
to say, 'Here's your secret!' The light attacked
through the mismatched boards of the barn roof.
Rain was on the way, but that was days off.
The golden afterthoughts of hay, fodder,
and dried horse dung rose in the air to form
a message only a fatherless child could read.
Another wind blew last night, the same wind
through the same cedars that welcomed me
back from madness thirty years ago and brought

the blessing I required. The wind can do that,
it can carry all the voices of the living
and the dead, but the dust holds its knowledge.

The dust said nothing on that morning
in 1933 when my father leaned his forehead down
on the steering wheel and spoke in Arabic
to tell me alone all he'd been and all
he would become. He loved those strange words.
He shouted the sudden plosives and the vowels
deep as moonlight and gave me each word
a second time as he took my hand in his
for the long moment until the traffic light
on Grand River turned from red to green
so we could enter the past. Since then I've misplaced
that tiny ideogram of his life etched in dust.
In its stead I have the Atlas cedar and the aspen
carrying the wind's words, the scraps
fluttering from the garbage – newspapers
stamped with no truths – a single mockingbird
rehearsing his psalms, and over the back fence
the scattered omens that rehearse the future,
a scum of graying clouds off the plating plant
garbling the constant message of the dead.

Call It Music

Some days I catch a rhythm, almost a song
in my own breath. I'm alone here
in Brooklyn Heights, late morning, the sky
above the St George Hotel clear, clear
for New York, that is. The radio playing
Bird Flight, Parker in his California
tragic voice fifty years ago, his faltering
'Lover Man' just before he crashed into chaos.
I would guess that outside the recording studio
in Burbank the sun was high above the jacarandas,
it was late March, the worst of yesterday's rain
had come and gone, the sky washed blue. Bird
could have seen for miles if he'd looked, but what
he saw was so foreign he clenched his eyes,
shook his head, and barked like a dog – just once –
and then Howard McGhee took his arm and assured him
he'd be OK. I know this because Howard told me
years later that he thought Bird could
lie down in the hotel room they shared, sleep
for an hour or more, and waken as himself.
The perfect sunlight angles into my little room
above Willow Street. I listen to my breath
come and go and try to catch its curious taste,
part milk, part iron, part blood, as it passes
from me into the world. This is not me,
this is automatic, this entering and exiting,
my body's essential occupation without which
I am a thing. The whole process has a name,
a word I don't know, an elegant word not
in English or Yiddish or Spanish, a word
that means nothing to me. Howard truly believed
what he said that day when he steered
Parker into a cab and drove the silent miles
beside him while the bright world
unfurled around them: filling stations, stands
of fruits and vegetables, a kiosk selling trinkets
from Mexico and the Philippines. It was all
so actual and Western, it was a new creation
coming into being, like the music of Charlie Parker
someone later called 'glad', though that day
I would have said silent, 'the silent music
of Charlie Parker'. Howard said nothing.
He paid the driver and helped Bird up two flights

to their room, got his boots off, and went out
to let him sleep as the afternoon entered
the history of darkness. I'm not judging
Howard, he did better than I could have
now or then. Then I was nineteen, working
on the loading docks at Railway Express
coming day by day into the damaged body
of a man while I sang into the filthy air
the Yiddish drinking songs my Zadie taught me
before his breath failed. Now Howard is gone,
eleven long years gone, the sweet voice silenced.
'The subtle bridge between Eldridge and Navarro,'
they later wrote, all that rising passion
a footnote to others. I remember in '85
walking the halls of Cass Tech, the high school
where he taught after his performing days,
when suddenly he took my left hand in his
two hands to tell me it all worked out
for the best. Maybe he'd gotten religion,
maybe he knew how little time was left,
maybe that day he was just worn down
by my questions about Parker. To him Bird
was truly Charlie Parker, a man, a silent note
going out forever on the breath of genius
which now I hear soaring above my own breath
as this bright morning fades into afternoon.
Music, I'll call it music. It's what we need
as the sun staggers behind the low gray clouds
blowing relentlessly in from that nameless ocean,
the calm and endless one I've still to cross.